DUMPED

written and illustrated by
andi watson

book design by
keith wood

edited by
jamie s. rich

published by
joe nozemack

Woodercaps Font designed by
woodrow phoenix

FOR CLARA

The author would also like to thank Paul Gravett and Ilya for getting me involved in the first place; Wds for the use of the font; Aphrodite, Judith and Sara at BIG for all their help; and Phil for working wonders with the initial proposal and her constant love and support (thanks, Hon).

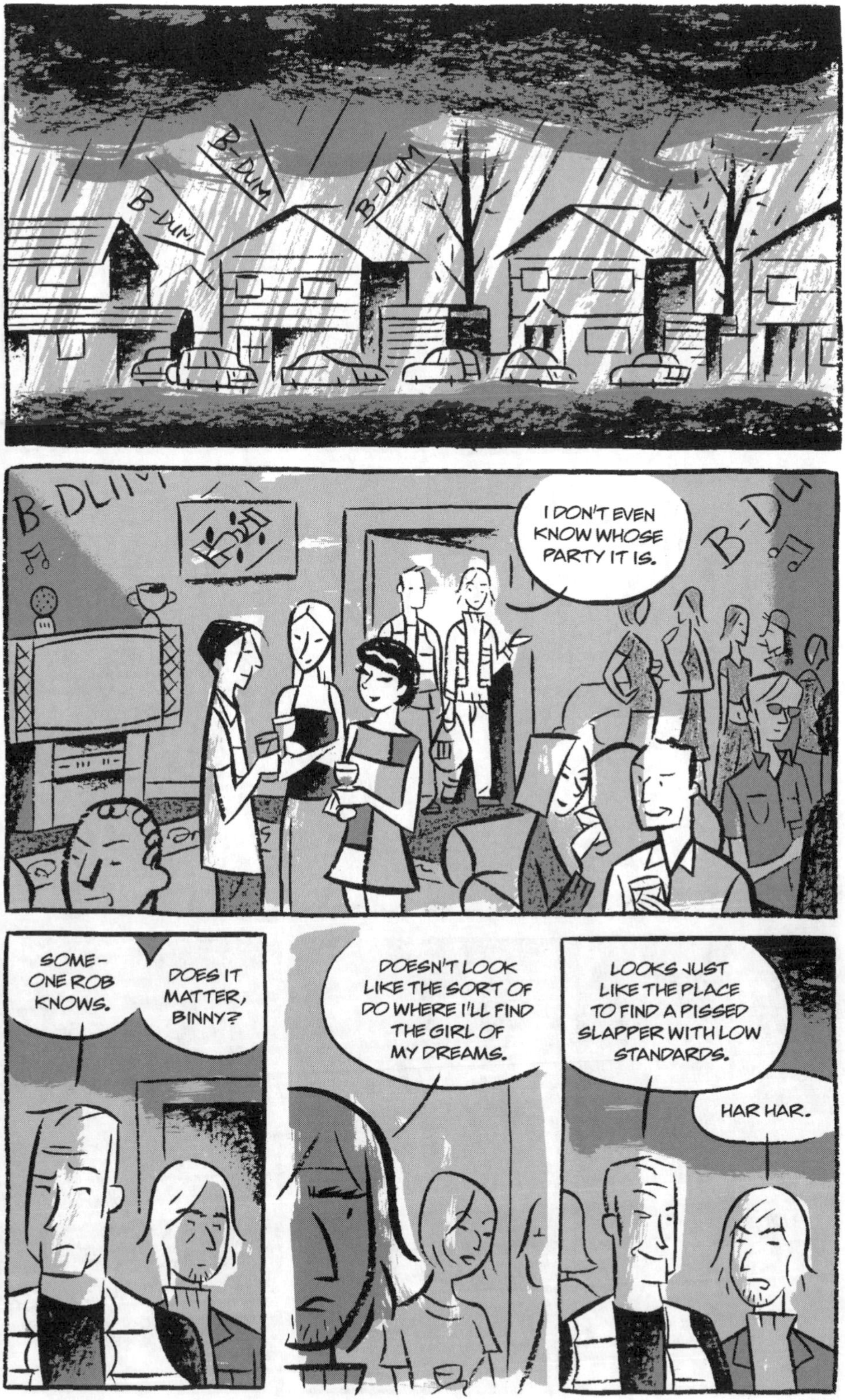
B-DUM
B-DUM
B-DUM
B-DUM
B-DUM
I DON'T EVEN KNOW WHOSE PARTY IT IS.
B-DU
SOME-ONE ROB KNOWS.
DOES IT MATTER, BINNY?
DOESN'T LOOK LIKE THE SORT OF DO WHERE I'LL FIND THE GIRL OF MY DREAMS.
LOOKS JUST LIKE THE PLACE TO FIND A PISSED SLAPPER WITH LOW STANDARDS.
HAR HAR.

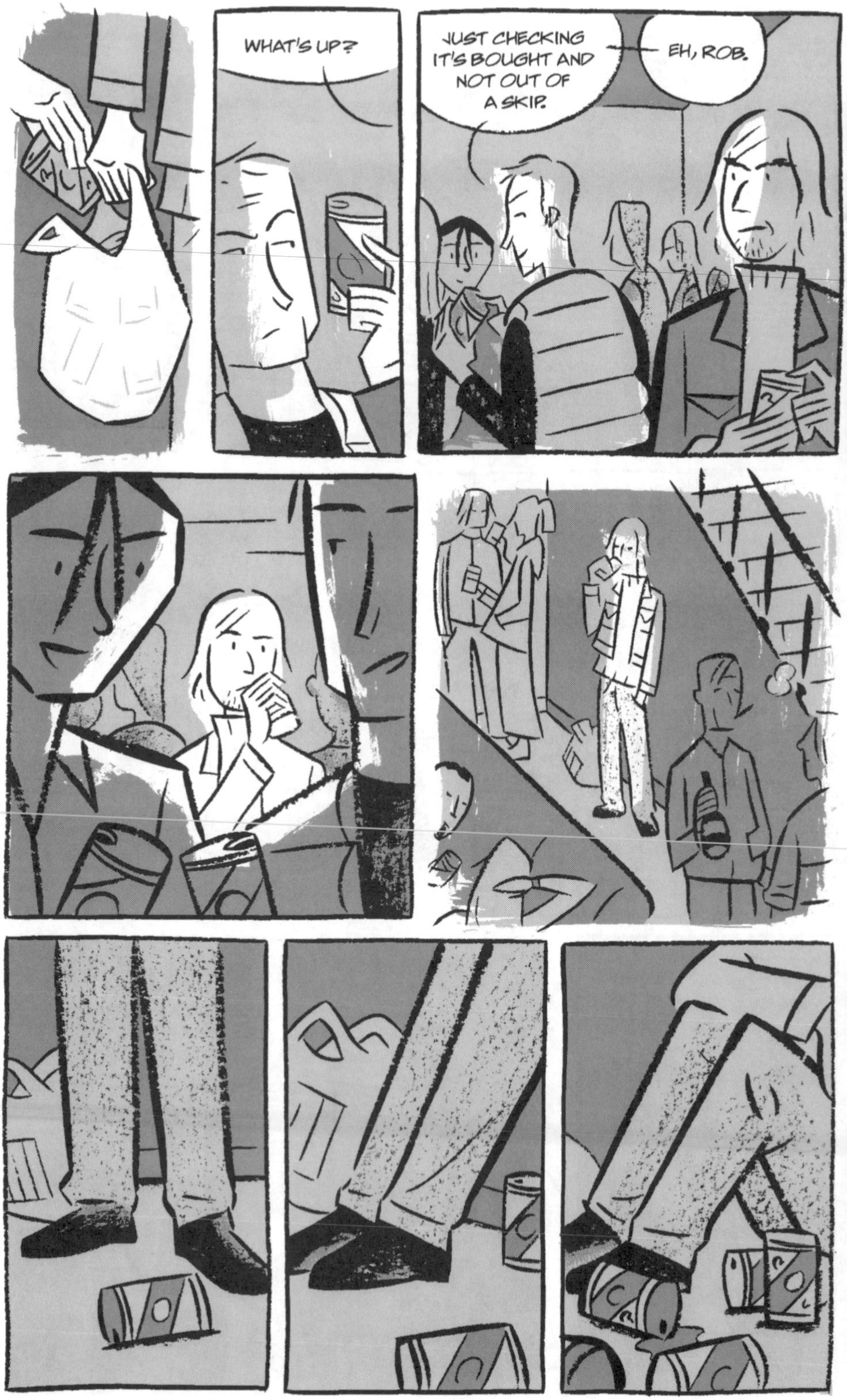
WHAT'S UP?
JUST CHECKING IT'S BOUGHT AND NOT OUT OF A SKIP.
EH, ROB.

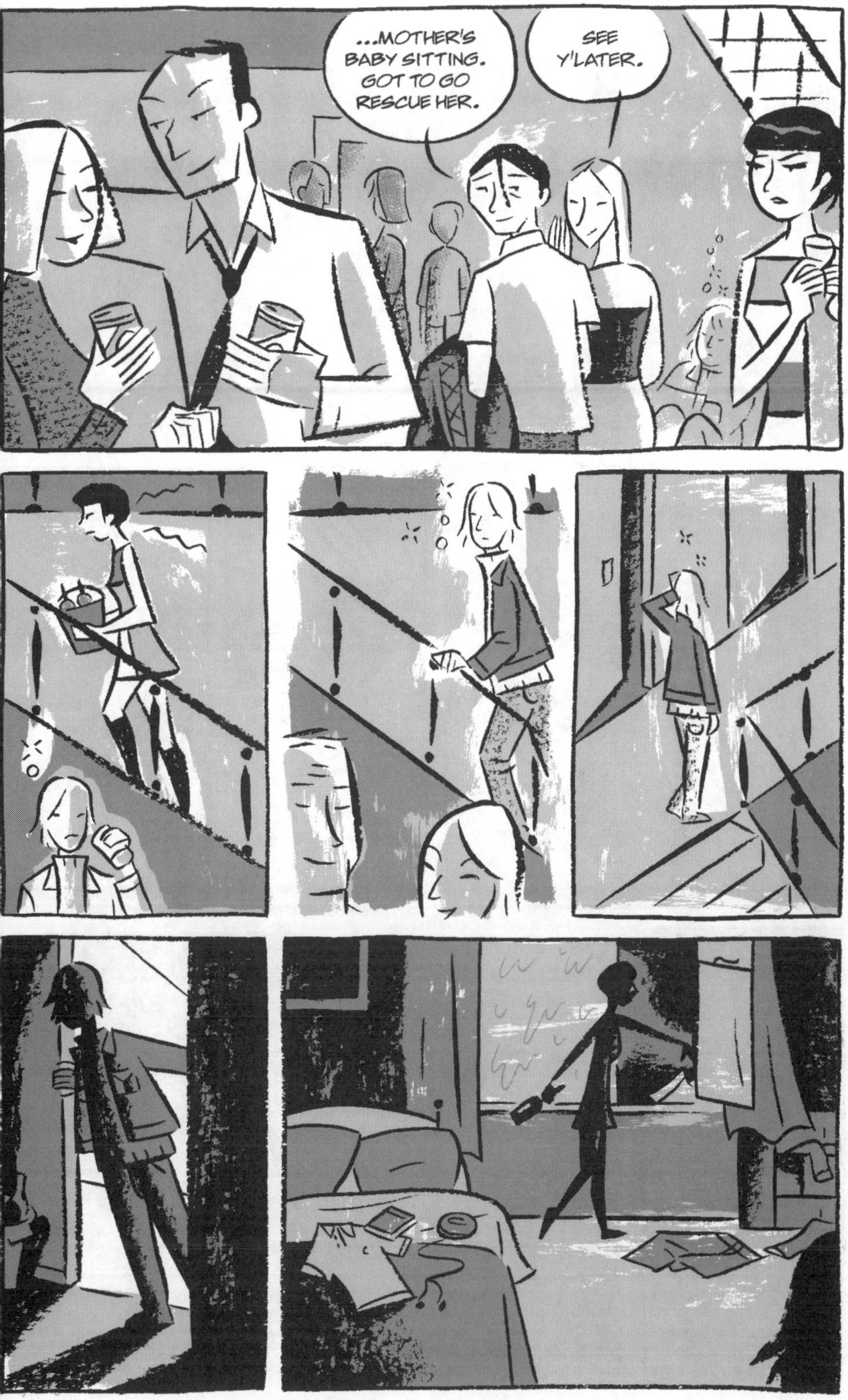
...MOTHER'S BABY SITTING. GOT TO GO RESCUE HER.
SEE Y'LATER.

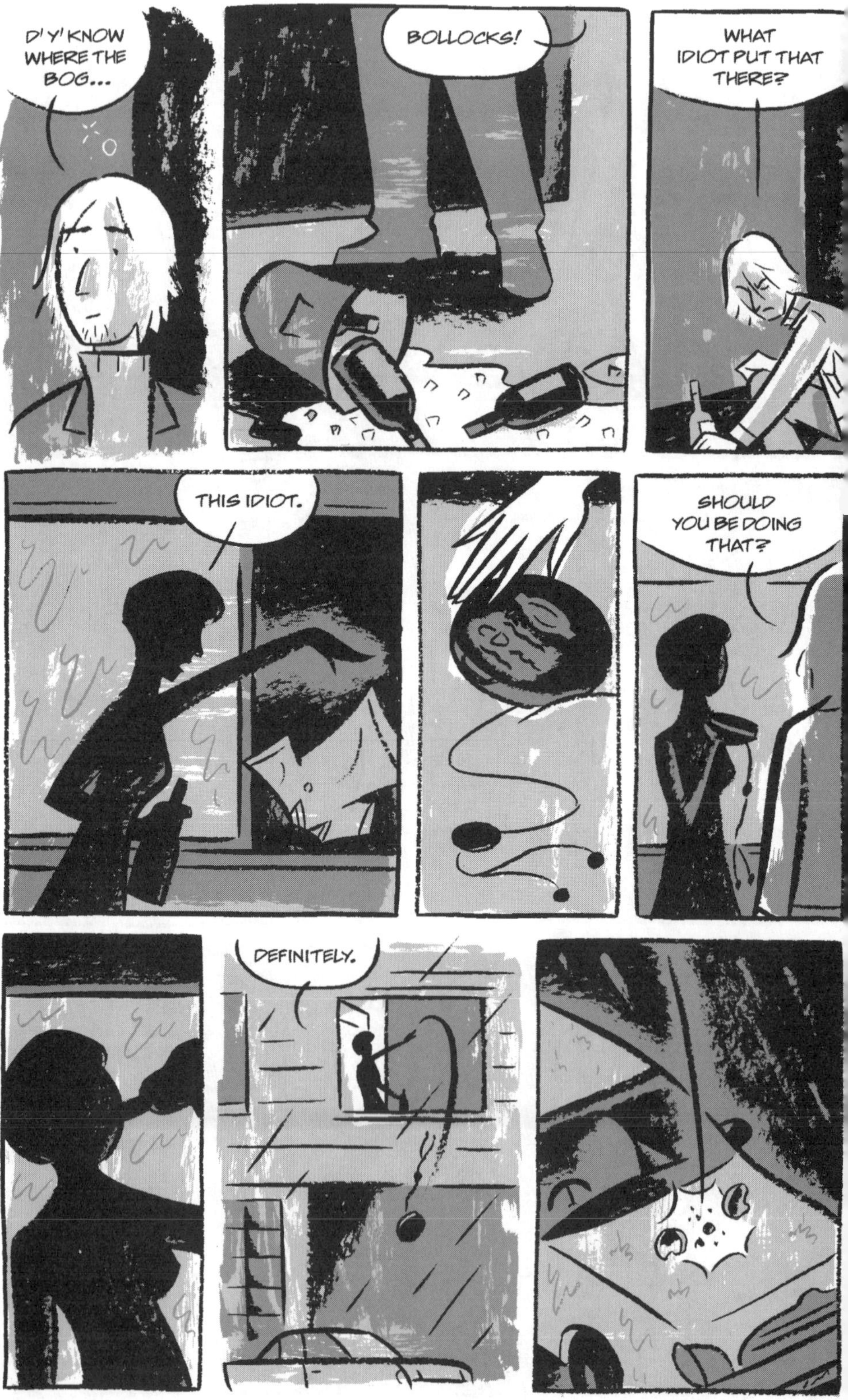
D' Y' KNOW WHERE THE BOG...
BOLLOCKS!
WHAT IDIOT PUT THAT THERE?
THIS IDIOT.
SHOULD YOU BE DOING THAT?
DEFINITELY.

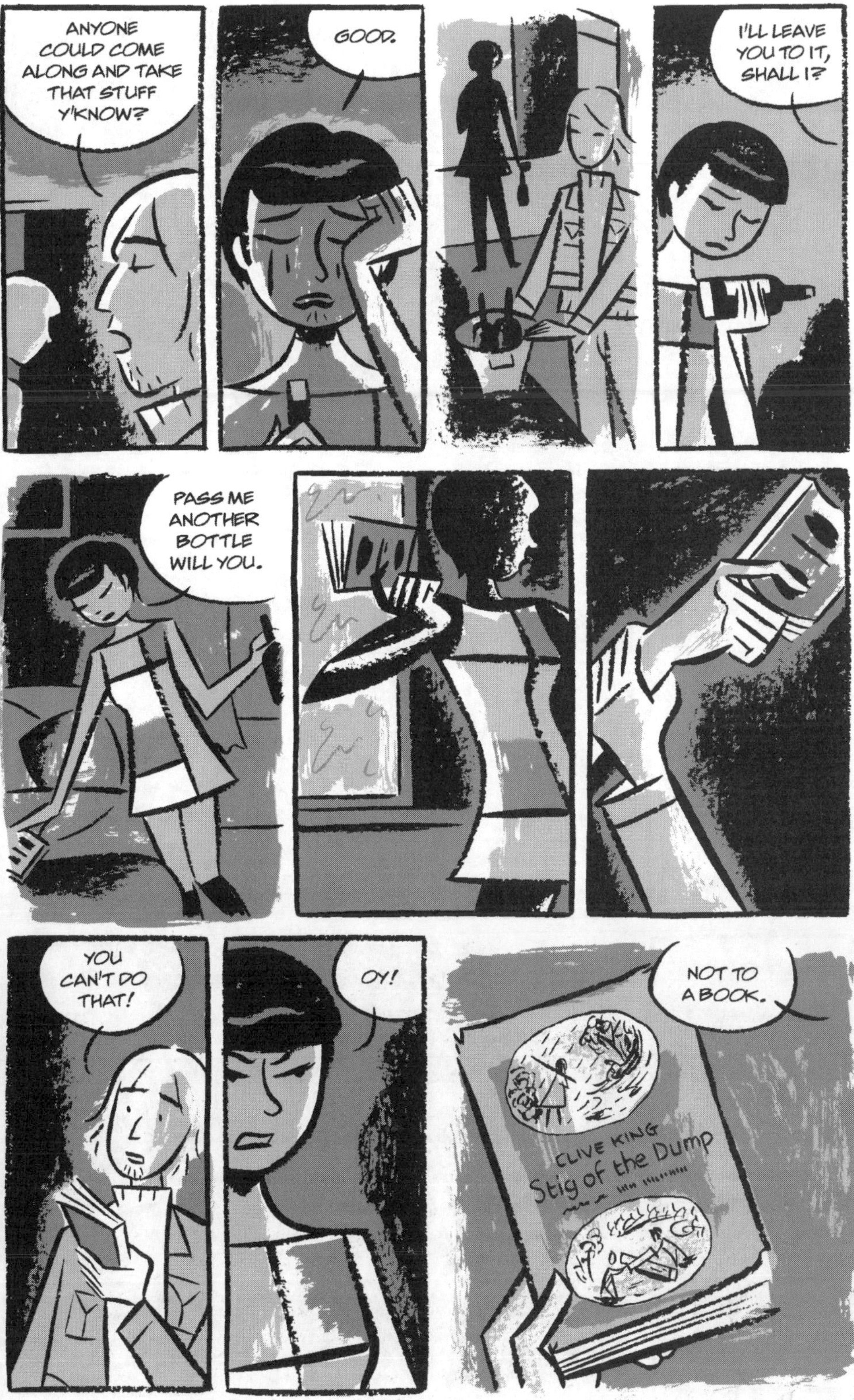
ANYONE COULD COME ALONG AND TAKE THAT STUFF Y'KNOW?
GOOD.
I'LL LEAVE YOU TO IT, SHALL I?
PASS ME ANOTHER BOTTLE WILL YOU.
YOU CAN'T DO THAT!
OY!
NOT TO A BOOK.
CLIVE KING
Stig of the Dump

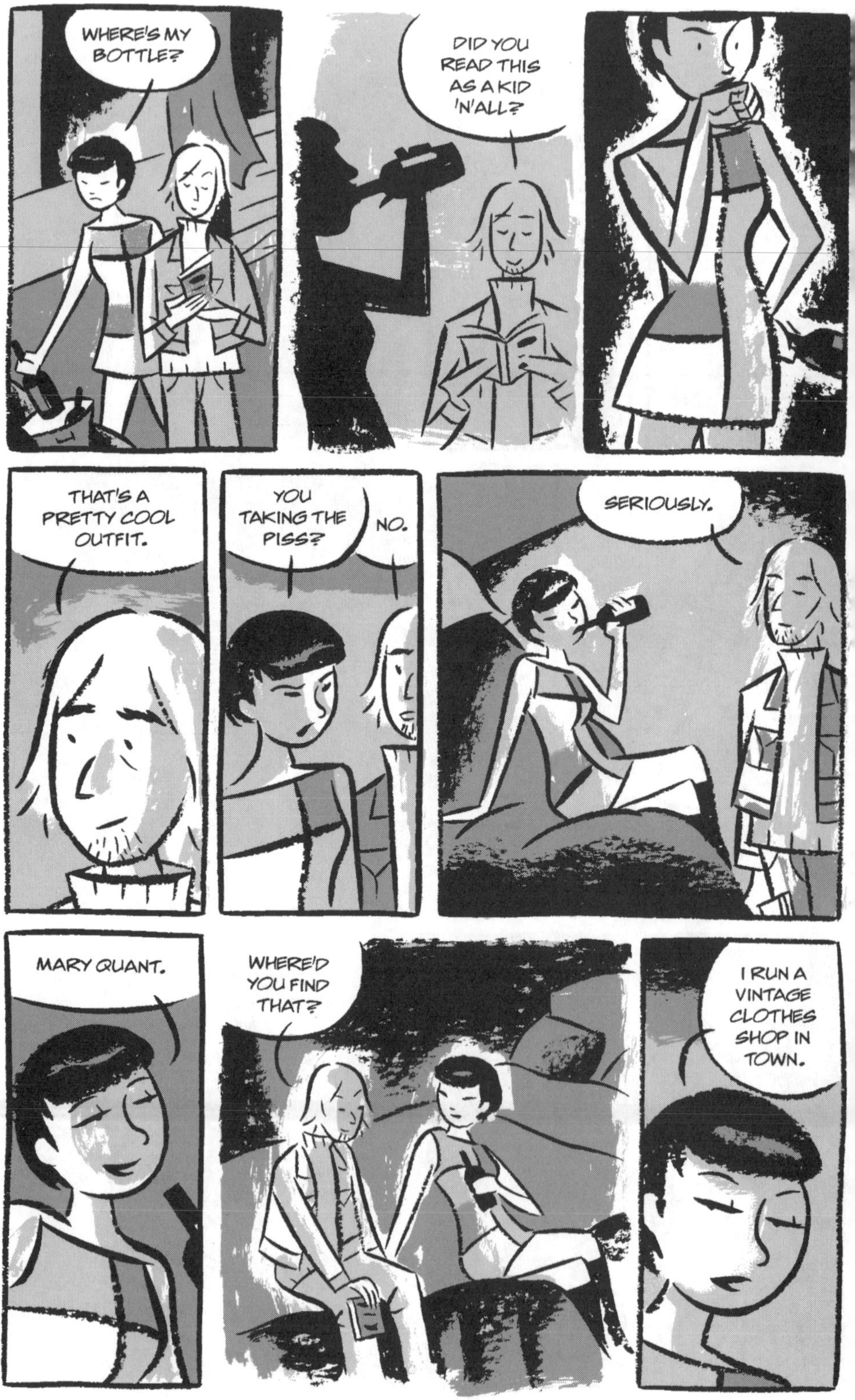
WHERE'S MY BOTTLE?
DID YOU READ THIS AS A KID 'N'ALL?
THAT'S A PRETTY COOL OUTFIT.
YOU TAKING THE PISS?
NO.
SERIOUSLY.
MARY QUANT.
WHERE'D YOU FIND THAT?
I RUN A VINTAGE CLOTHES SHOP IN TOWN.

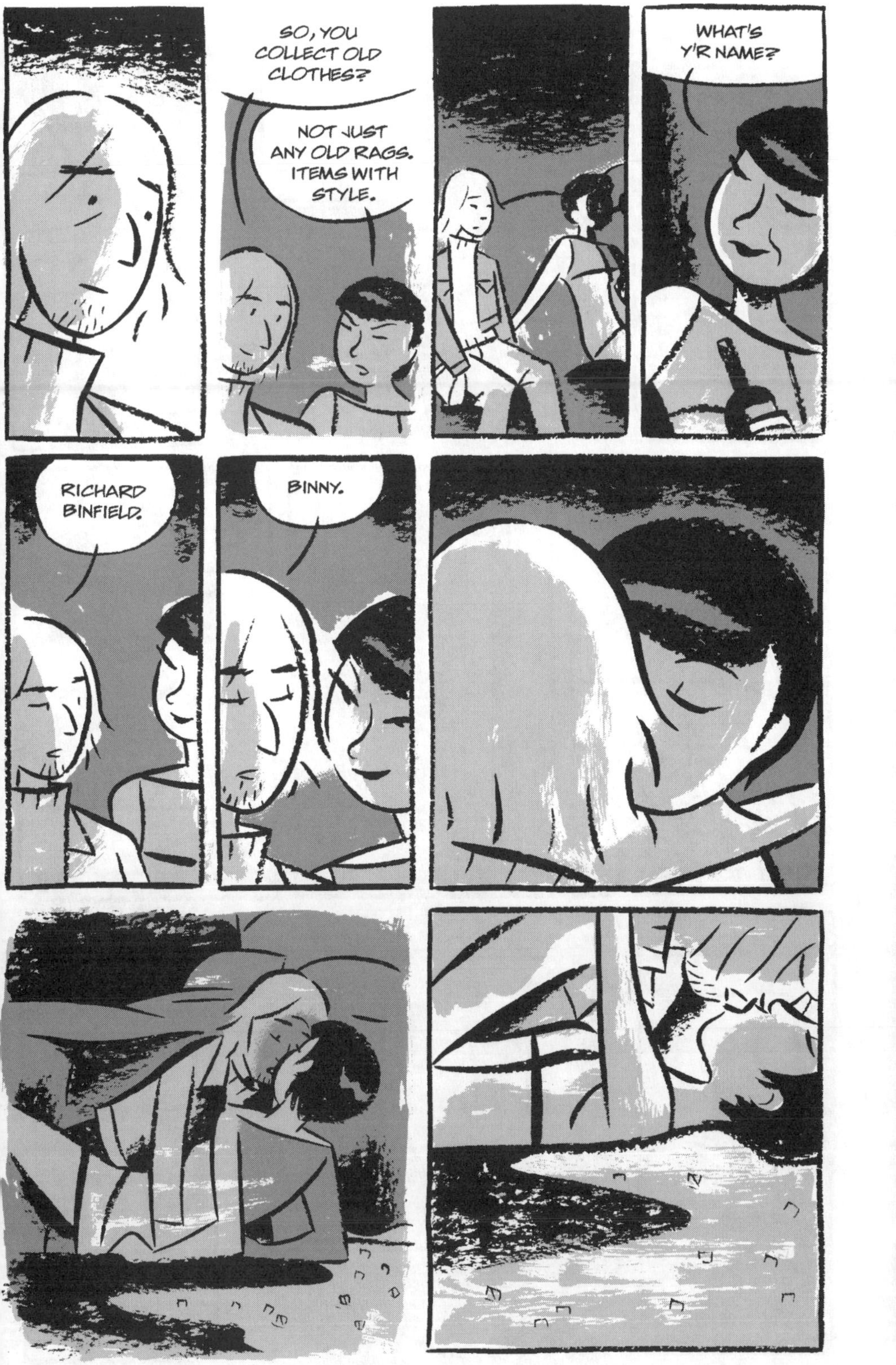
SO, YOU COLLECT OLD CLOTHES?
NOT JUST ANY OLD RAGS. ITEMS WITH STYLE.
WHAT'S Y'R NAME?
RICHARD BINFIELD.
BINNY.

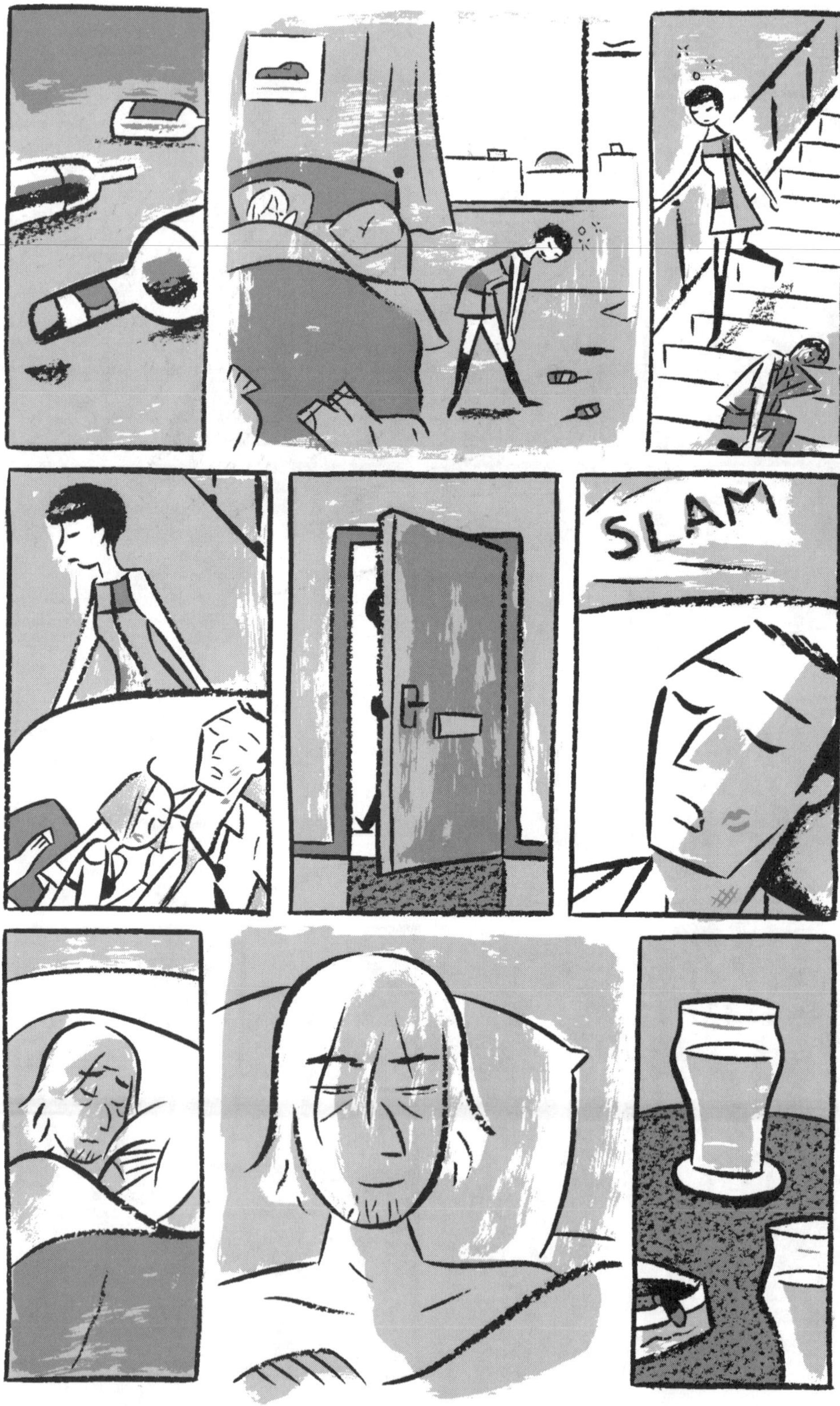
SLAM

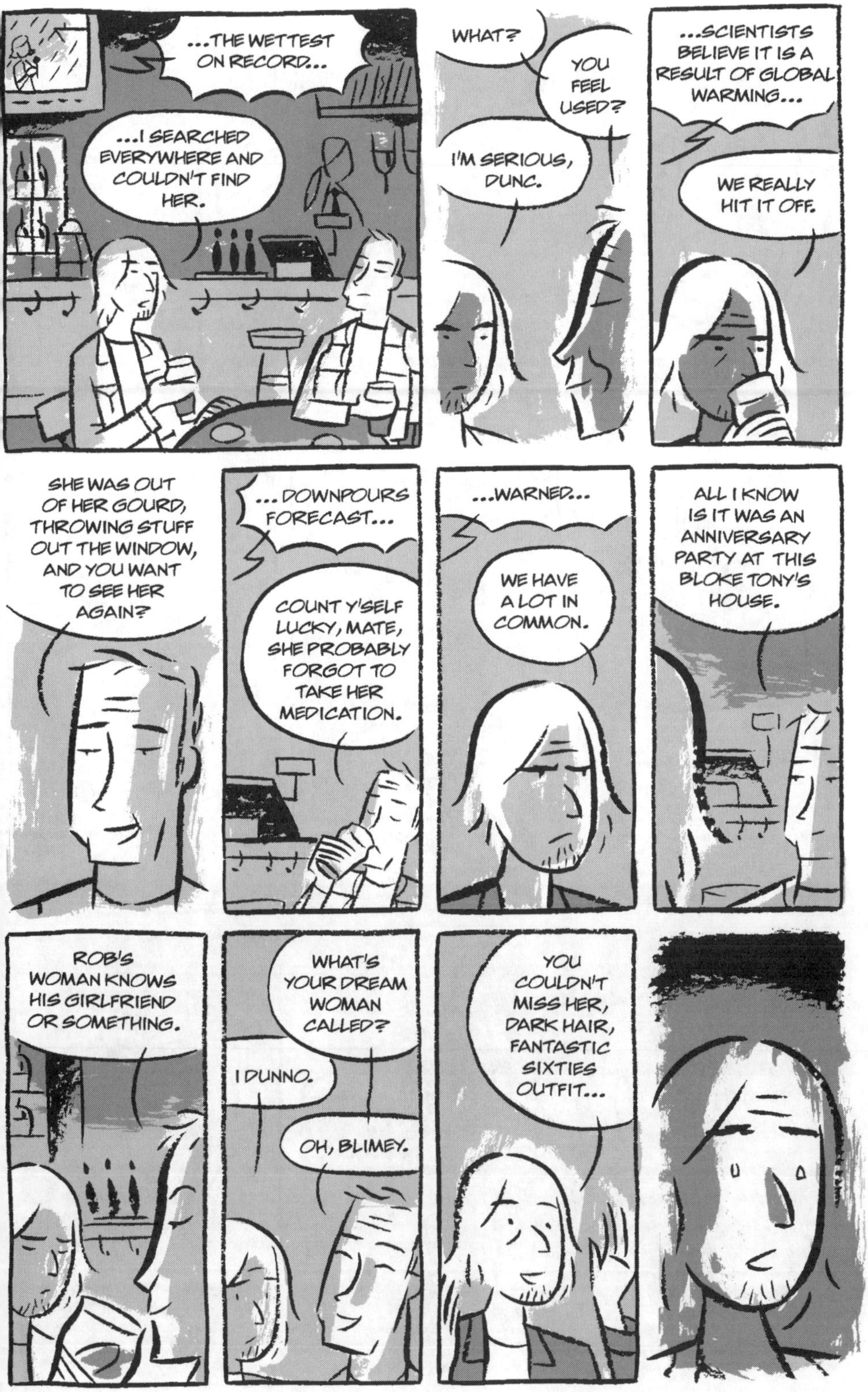
...THE WETTEST ON RECORD...
...I SEARCHED EVERYWHERE AND COULDN'T FIND HER.
WHAT?
YOU FEEL USED?
I'M SERIOUS, DUNC.
...SCIENTISTS BELIEVE IT IS A RESULT OF GLOBAL WARMING...
WE REALLY HIT IT OFF.
SHE WAS OUT OF HER GOURD, THROWING STUFF OUT THE WINDOW, AND YOU WANT TO SEE HER AGAIN?
... DOWNPOURS FORECAST...
COUNT Y'SELF LUCKY, MATE, SHE PROBABLY FORGOT TO TAKE HER MEDICATION.
...WARNED...
WE HAVE A LOT IN COMMON.
ALL I KNOW IS IT WAS AN ANNIVERSARY PARTY AT THIS BLOKE TONY'S HOUSE.
ROB'S WOMAN KNOWS HIS GIRLFRIEND OR SOMETHING.
WHAT'S YOUR DREAM WOMAN CALLED?
I DUNNO.
OH, BLIMEY.
YOU COULDN'T MISS HER, DARK HAIR, FANTASTIC SIXTIES OUTFIT...

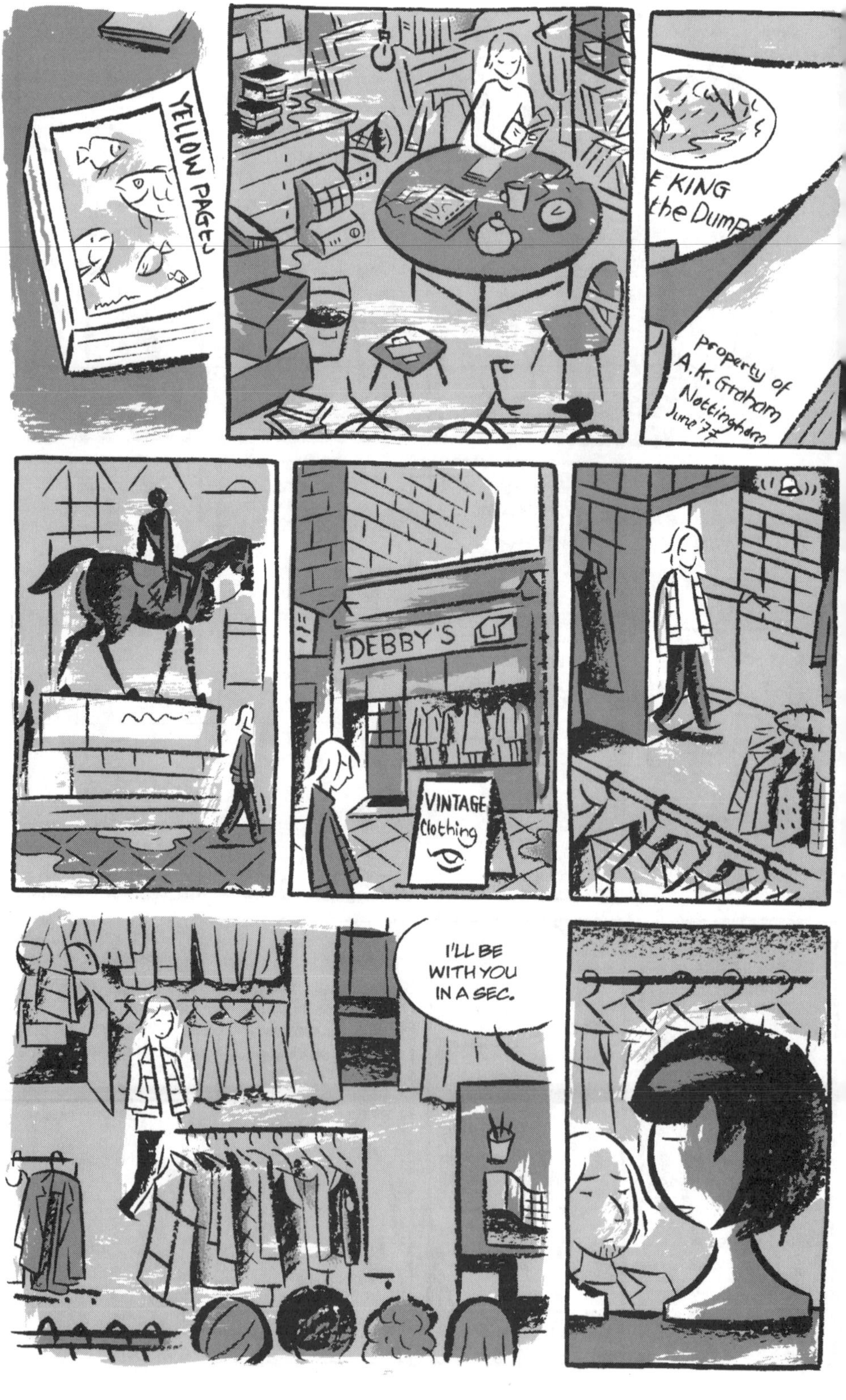
YELLOW PAGES
E KING
the Dump
Property of
A.K. Graham
Nottingham
June '77
DEBBY'S
VINTAGE
Clothing
I'LL BE
WITH YOU
IN A SEC.

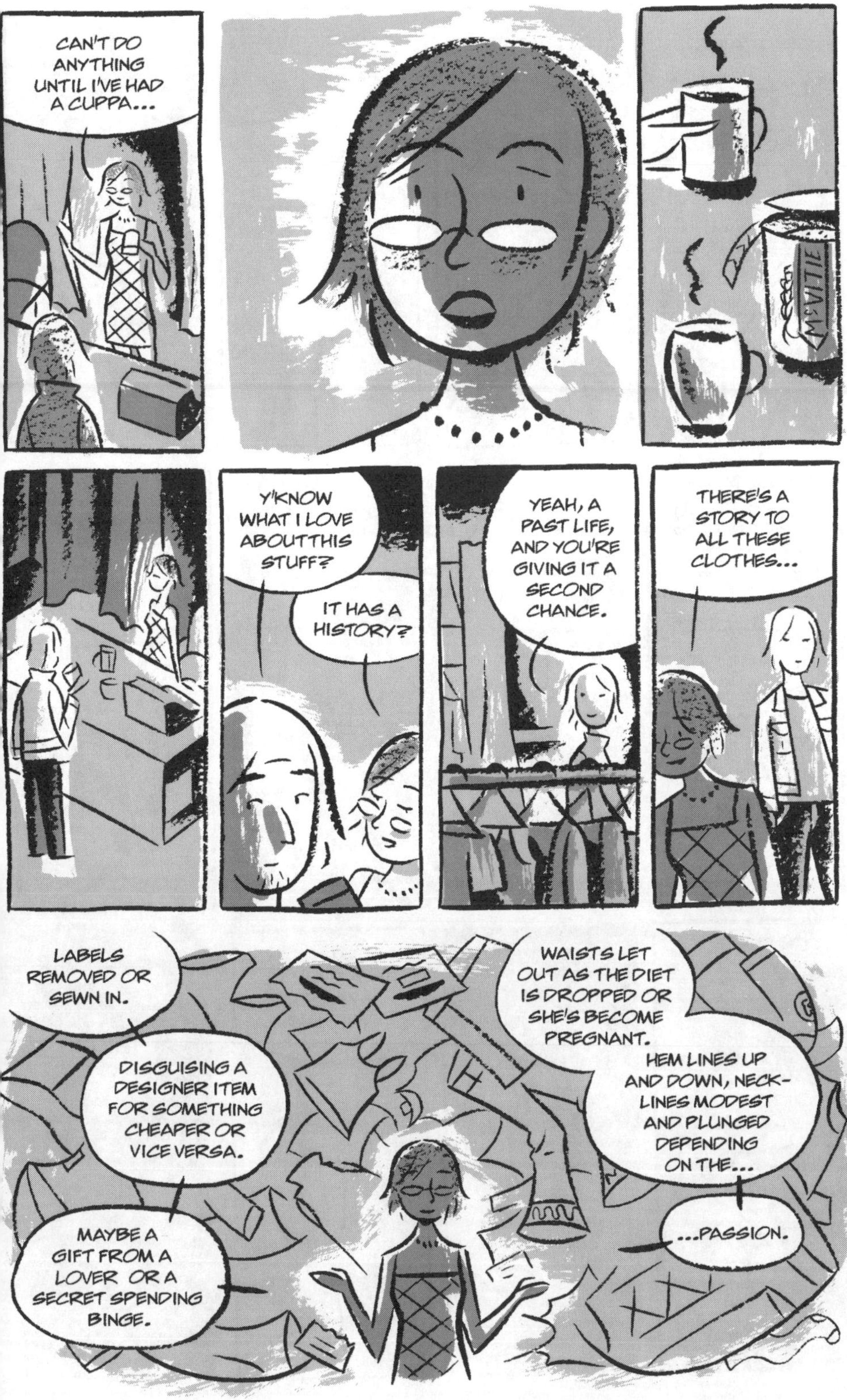
CAN'T DO ANYTHING UNTIL I'VE HAD A CUPPA...
McVITIE
Y'KNOW WHAT I LOVE ABOUT THIS STUFF?
IT HAS A HISTORY?
YEAH, A PAST LIFE, AND YOU'RE GIVING IT A SECOND CHANCE.
THERE'S A STORY TO ALL THESE CLOTHES...
LABELS REMOVED OR SEWN IN.
DISGUISING A DESIGNER ITEM FOR SOMETHING CHEAPER OR VICE VERSA.
MAYBE A GIFT FROM A LOVER OR A SECRET SPENDING BINGE.
WAISTS LET OUT AS THE DIET IS DROPPED OR SHE'S BECOME PREGNANT.
HEM LINES UP AND DOWN, NECK-LINES MODEST AND PLUNGED DEPENDING ON THE...
...PASSION.

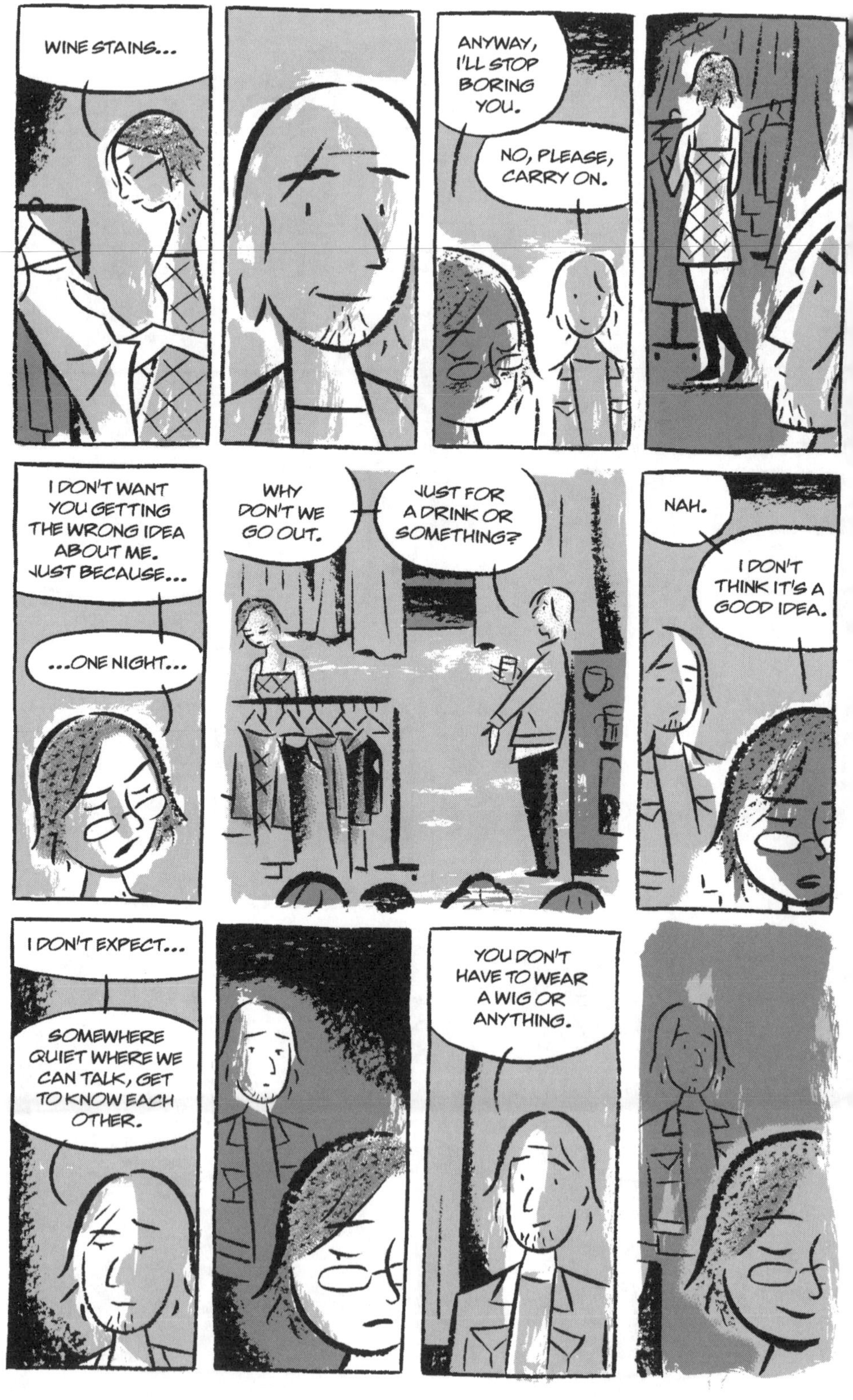
WINE STAINS...
ANYWAY, I'LL STOP BORING YOU.
NO, PLEASE, CARRY ON.
I DON'T WANT YOU GETTING THE WRONG IDEA ABOUT ME. JUST BECAUSE...
...ONE NIGHT...
WHY DON'T WE GO OUT.
JUST FOR A DRINK OR SOMETHING?
NAH.
I DON'T THINK IT'S A GOOD IDEA.
I DON'T EXPECT...
SOMEWHERE QUIET WHERE WE CAN TALK, GET TO KNOW EACH OTHER.
YOU DON'T HAVE TO WEAR A WIG OR ANYTHING.

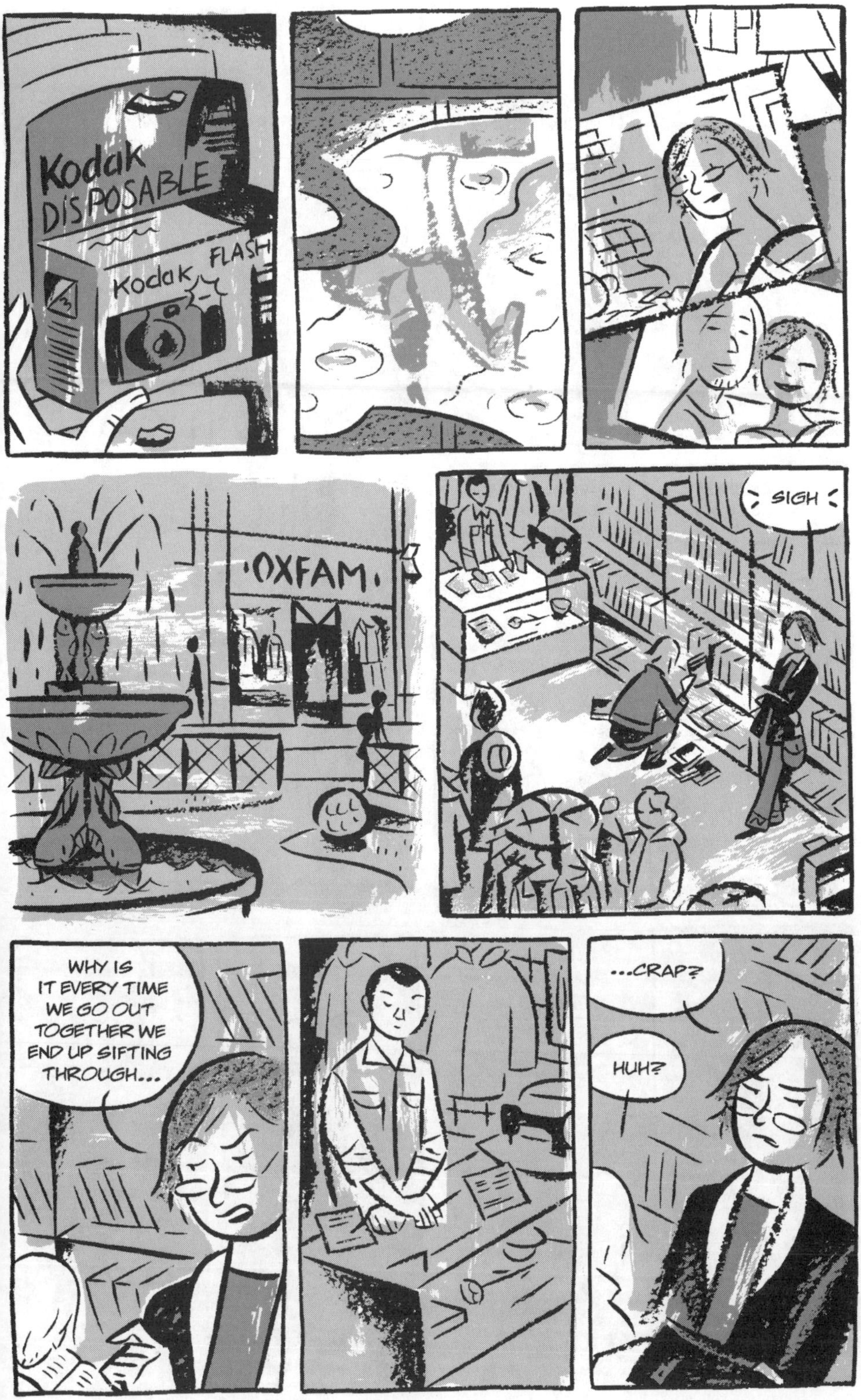

Kodak
DISPOSABLE
Kodak
FLASH
OXFAM
SIGH
WHY IS IT EVERY TIME WE GO OUT TOGETHER WE END UP SIFTING THROUGH...
...CRAP?
HUH?

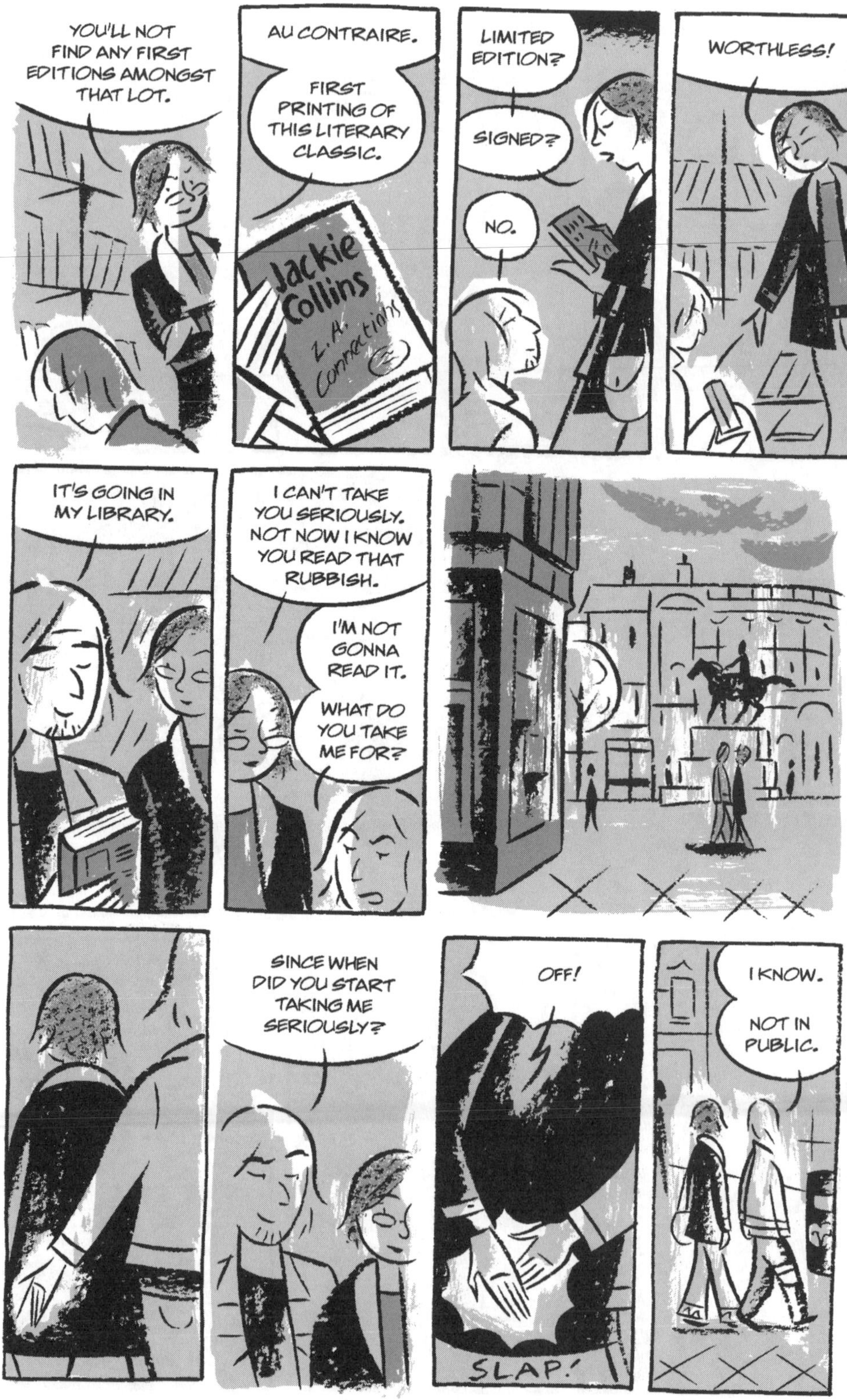
YOU'LL NOT FIND ANY FIRST EDITIONS AMONGST THAT LOT.
AU CONTRAIRE.
FIRST PRINTING OF THIS LITERARY CLASSIC.
Jackie Collins
LIMITED EDITION?
SIGNED?
NO.
WORTHLESS!
IT'S GOING IN MY LIBRARY.
I CAN'T TAKE YOU SERIOUSLY. NOT NOW I KNOW YOU READ THAT RUBBISH.
I'M NOT GONNA READ IT.
WHAT DO YOU TAKE ME FOR?
SINCE WHEN DID YOU START TAKING ME SERIOUSLY?
OFF!
SLAP!
I KNOW.
NOT IN PUBLIC.

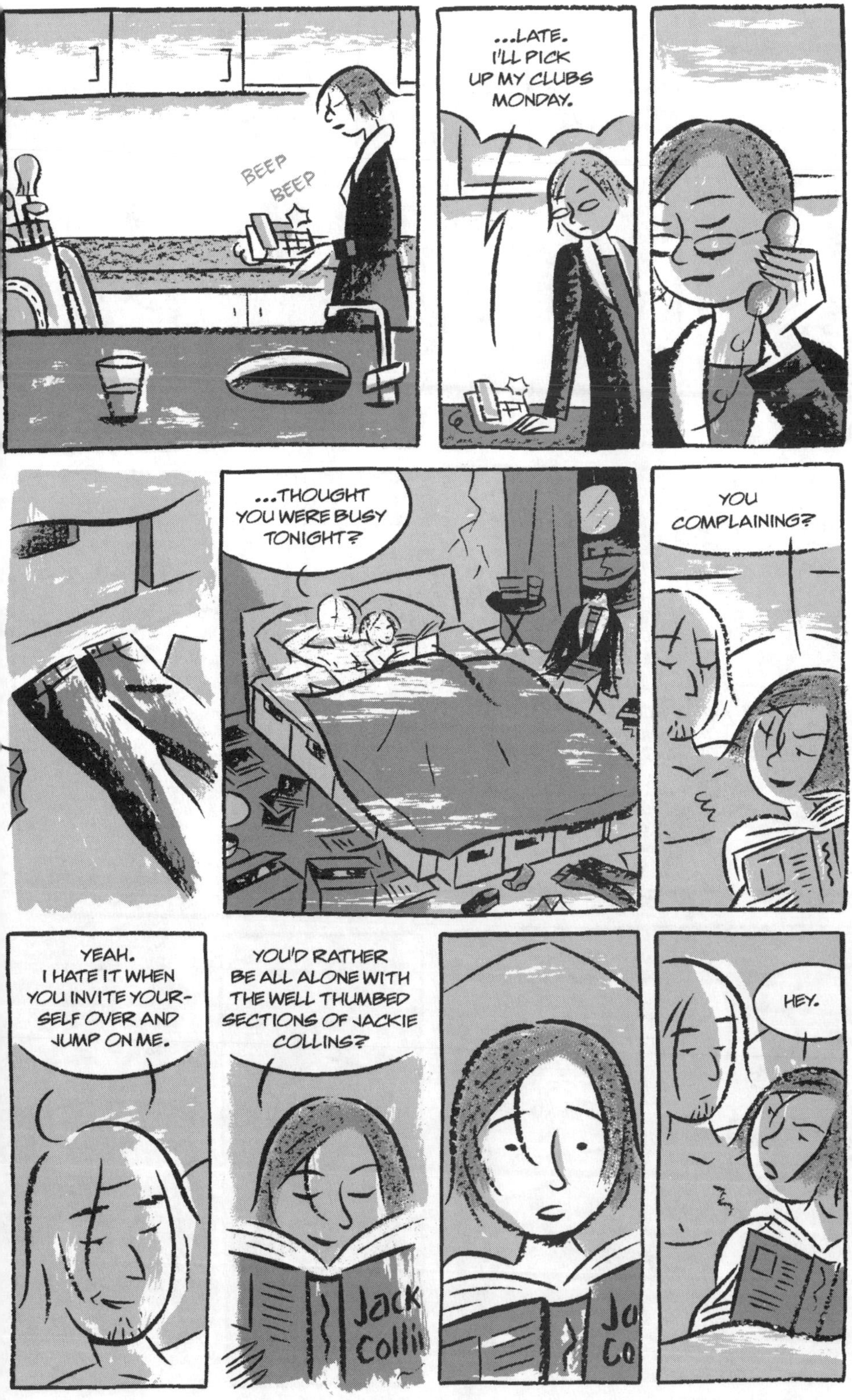
BEEP
BEEP
...LATE. I'LL PICK UP MY CLUBS MONDAY.
...THOUGHT YOU WERE BUSY TONIGHT?
YOU COMPLAINING?
YEAH. I HATE IT WHEN YOU INVITE YOURSELF OVER AND JUMP ON ME.
YOU'D RATHER BE ALL ALONE WITH THE WELL THUMBED SECTIONS OF JACKIE COLLINS?
Jack Colli
HEY.

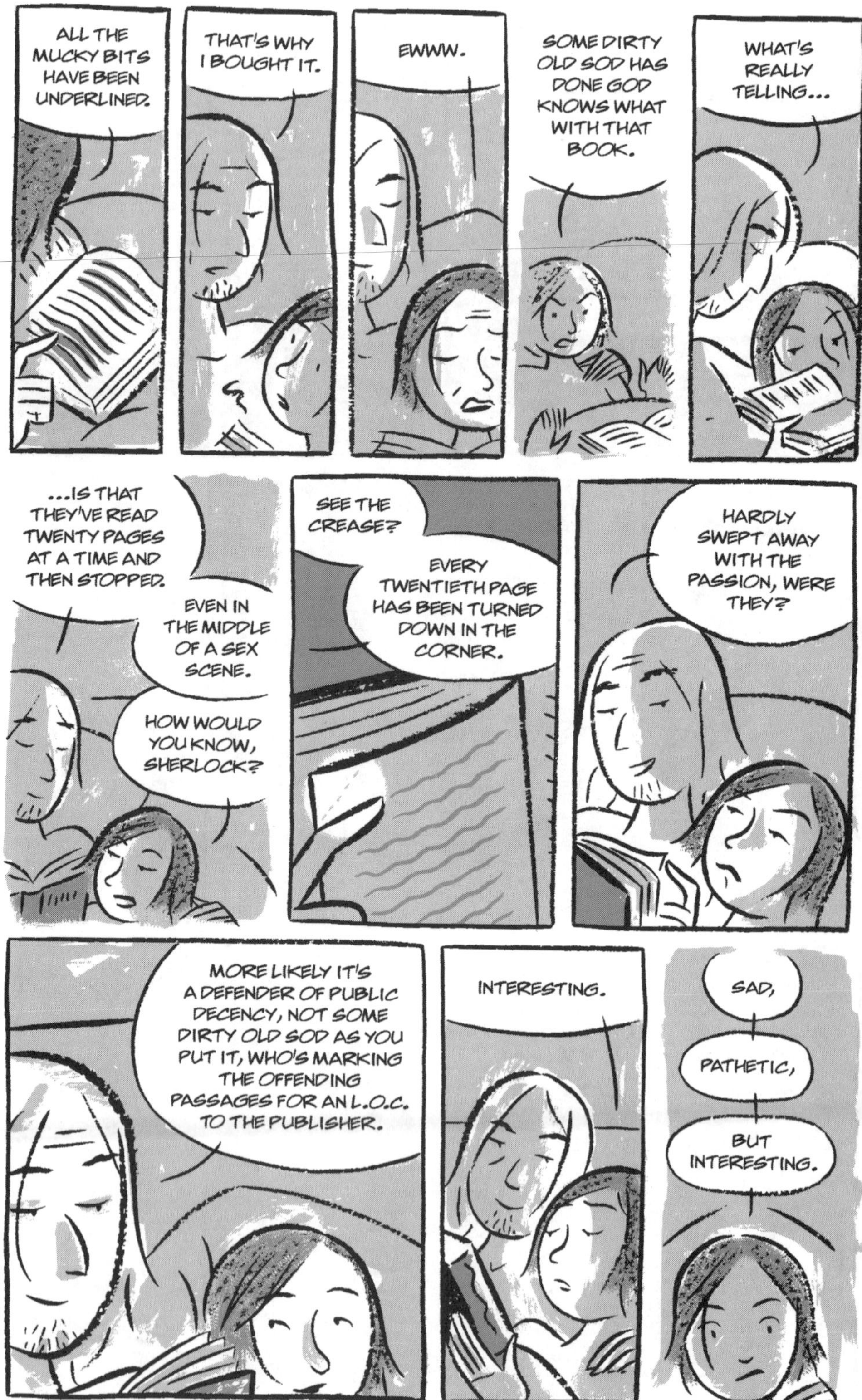
ALL THE MUCKY BITS HAVE BEEN UNDERLINED.
THAT'S WHY I BOUGHT IT.
EWWW.
SOME DIRTY OLD SOD HAS DONE GOD KNOWS WHAT WITH THAT BOOK.
WHAT'S REALLY TELLING...
...IS THAT THEY'VE READ TWENTY PAGES AT A TIME AND THEN STOPPED.
EVEN IN THE MIDDLE OF A SEX SCENE.
HOW WOULD YOU KNOW, SHERLOCK?
SEE THE CREASE?
EVERY TWENTIETH PAGE HAS BEEN TURNED DOWN IN THE CORNER.
HARDLY SWEPT AWAY WITH THE PASSION, WERE THEY?
MORE LIKELY IT'S A DEFENDER OF PUBLIC DECENCY, NOT SOME DIRTY OLD SOD AS YOU PUT IT, WHO'S MARKING THE OFFENDING PASSAGES FOR AN L.O.C. TO THE PUBLISHER.
INTERESTING.
SAD,
PATHETIC,
BUT INTERESTING.

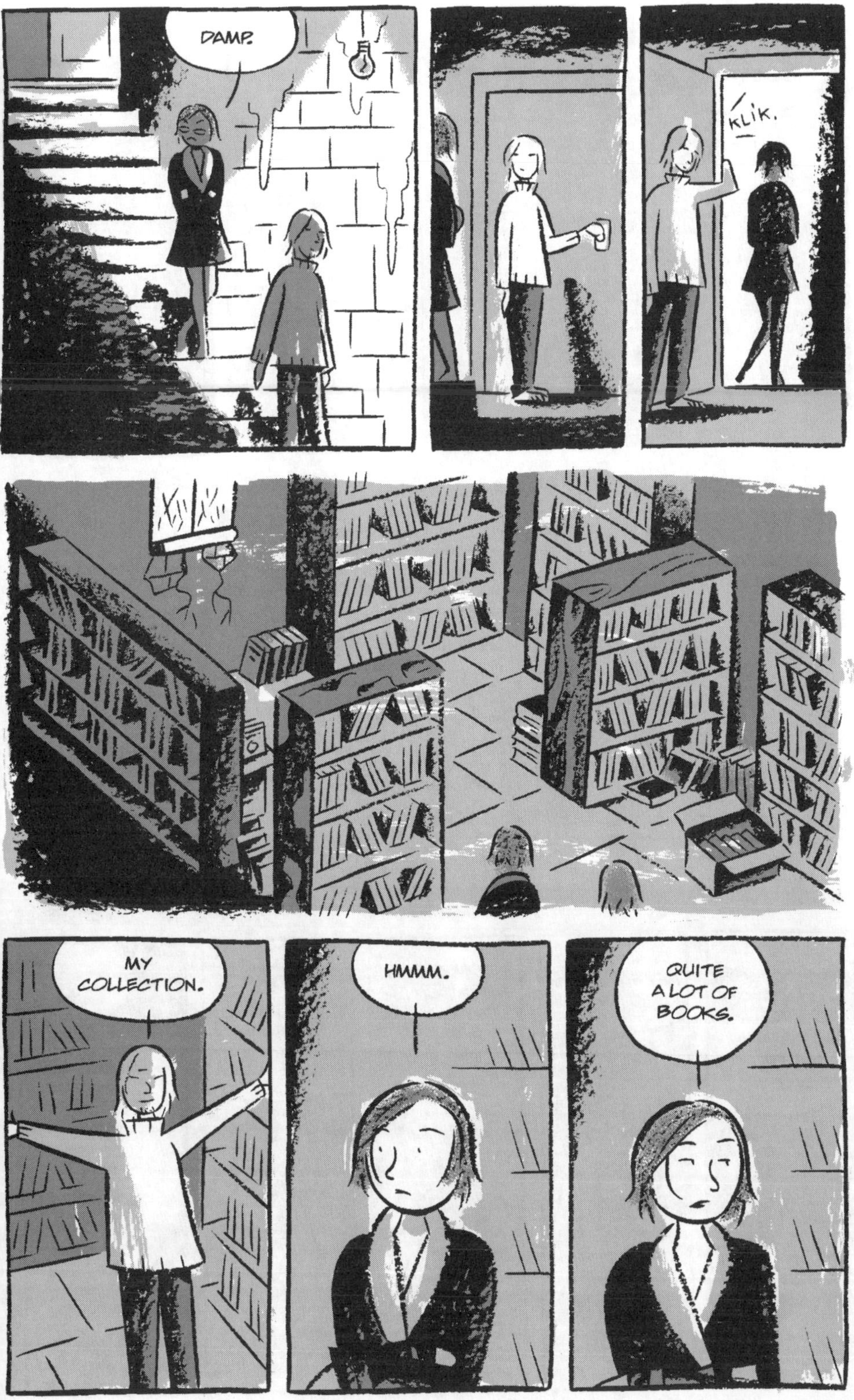
DAMP?
KLIK.
MY COLLECTION.
HMMM.
QUITE A LOT OF BOOKS.

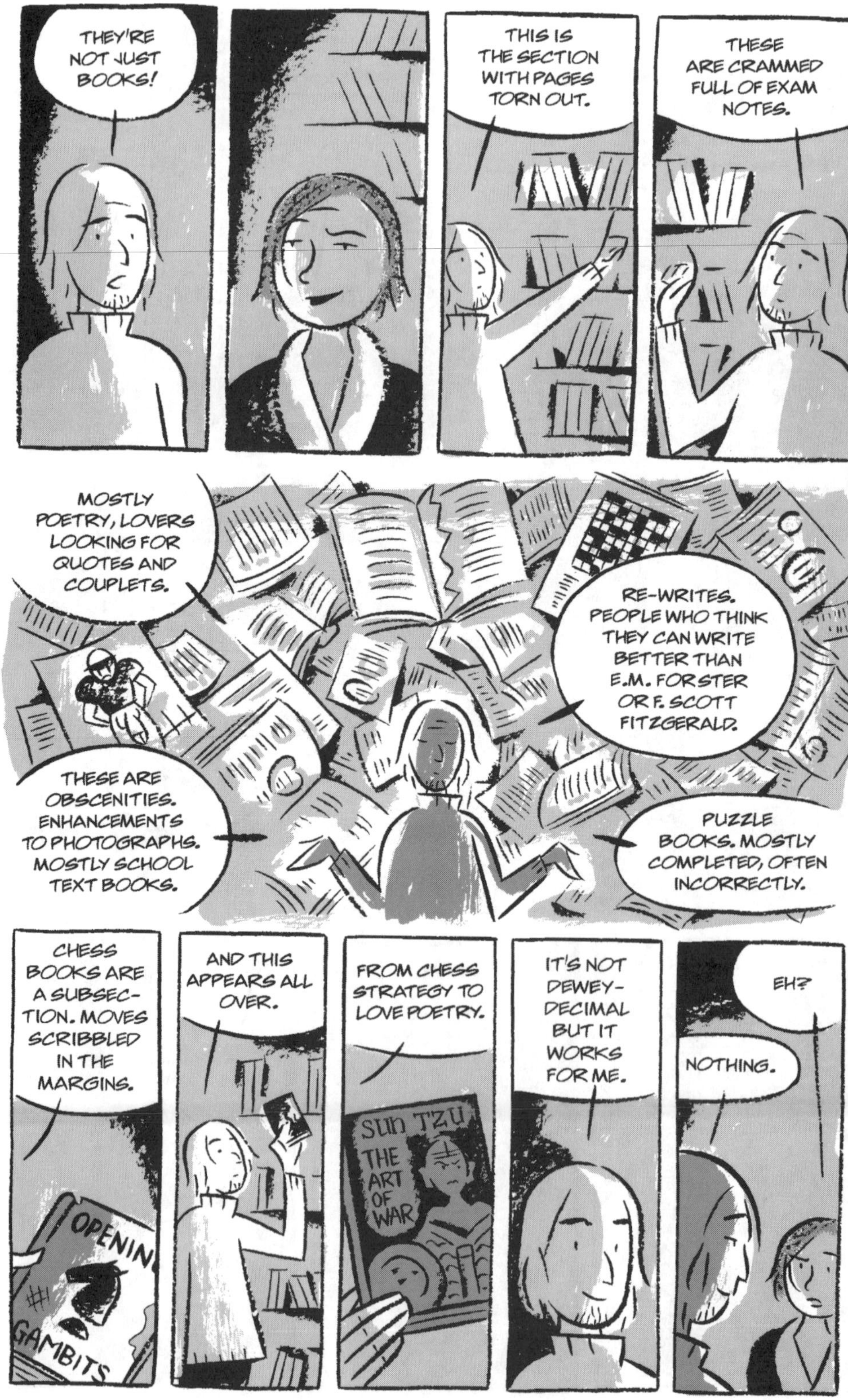
THEY'RE NOT JUST BOOKS!
THIS IS THE SECTION WITH PAGES TORN OUT.
THESE ARE CRAMMED FULL OF EXAM NOTES.
MOSTLY POETRY, LOVERS LOOKING FOR QUOTES AND COUPLETS.
RE-WRITES. PEOPLE WHO THINK THEY CAN WRITE BETTER THAN E.M. FORSTER OR F. SCOTT FITZGERALD.
THESE ARE OBSCENITIES. ENHANCEMENTS TO PHOTOGRAPHS. MOSTLY SCHOOL TEXT BOOKS.
PUZZLE BOOKS. MOSTLY COMPLETED, OFTEN INCORRECTLY.
CHESS BOOKS ARE A SUBSEC-TION. MOVES SCRIBBLED IN THE MARGINS.
OPENIN
GAMBITS
AND THIS APPEARS ALL OVER.
FROM CHESS STRATEGY TO LOVE POETRY.
SUN TZU
THE ART OF WAR
IT'S NOT DEWEY-DECIMAL BUT IT WORKS FOR ME.
EH?
NOTHING.

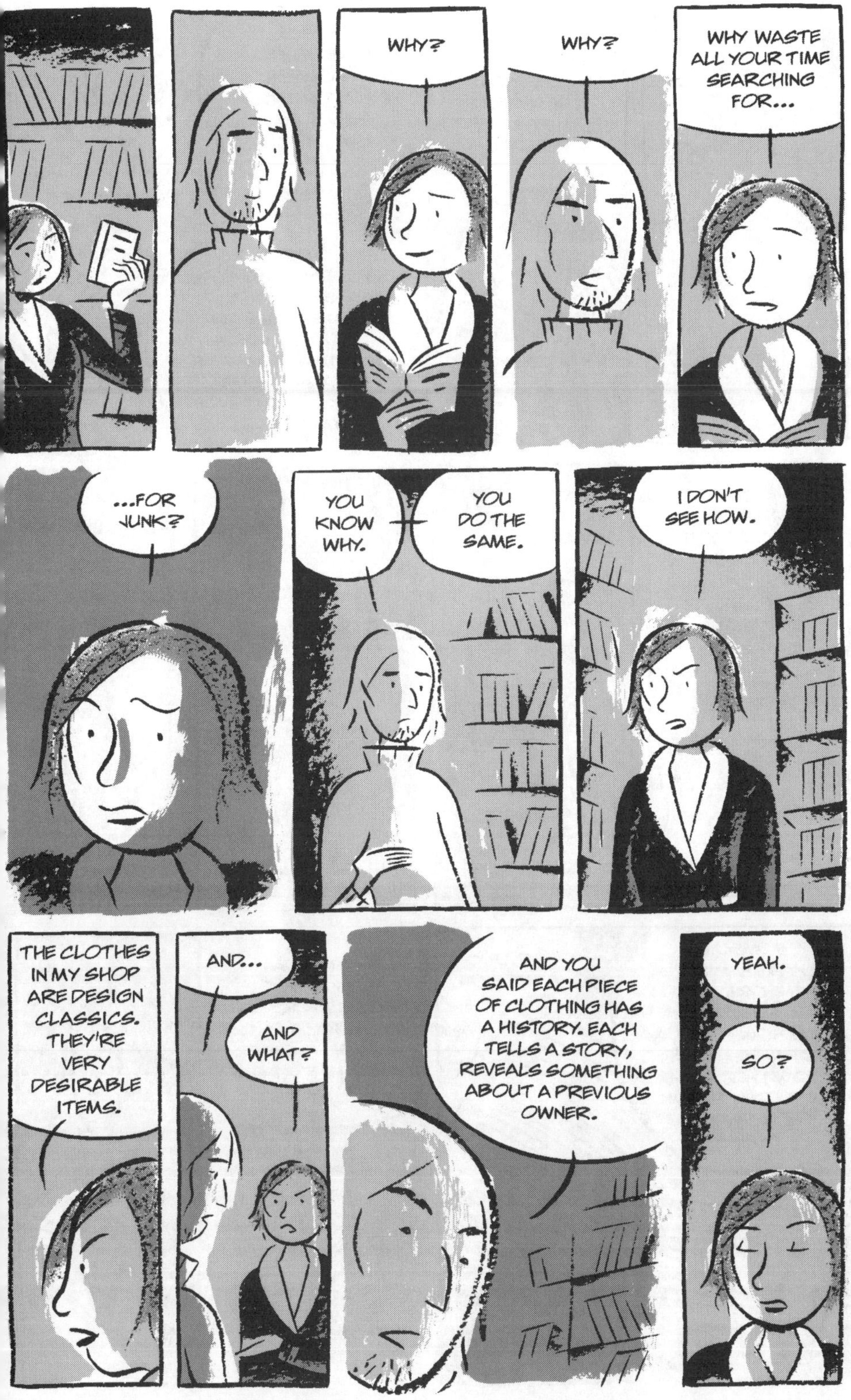
WHY?
WHY?
WHY WASTE ALL YOUR TIME SEARCHING FOR...
...FOR JUNK?
YOU KNOW WHY.
YOU DO THE SAME.
I DON'T SEE HOW.
THE CLOTHES IN MY SHOP ARE DESIGN CLASSICS. THEY'RE VERY DESIRABLE ITEMS.
AND...
AND WHAT?
AND YOU SAID EACH PIECE OF CLOTHING HAS A HISTORY. EACH TELLS A STORY, REVEALS SOMETHING ABOUT A PREVIOUS OWNER.
YEAH.
SO?

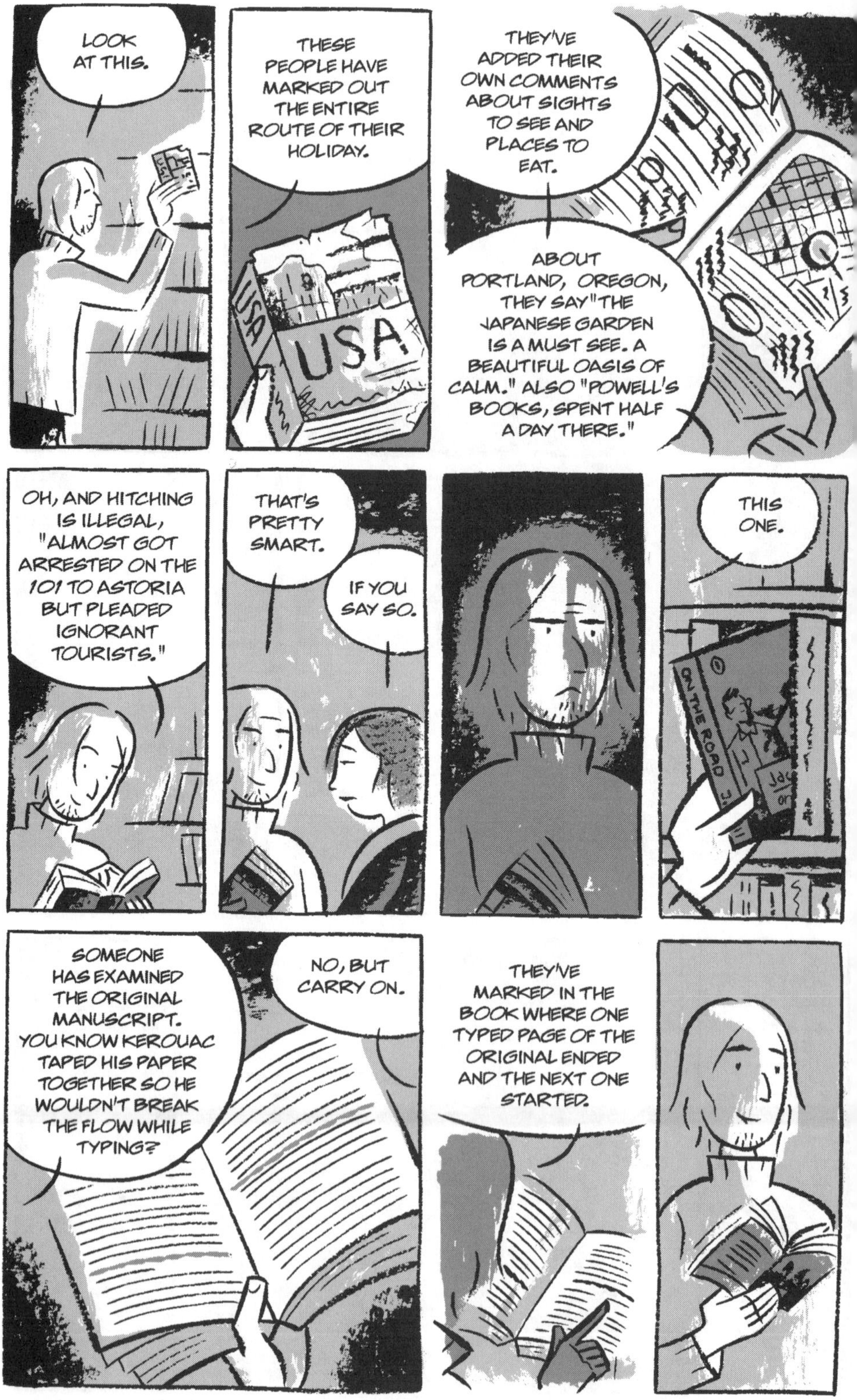
LOOK AT THIS.
THESE PEOPLE HAVE MARKED OUT THE ENTIRE ROUTE OF THEIR HOLIDAY.
USA
USA
THEY'VE ADDED THEIR OWN COMMENTS ABOUT SIGHTS TO SEE AND PLACES TO EAT.
ABOUT PORTLAND, OREGON, THEY SAY "THE JAPANESE GARDEN IS A MUST SEE. A BEAUTIFUL OASIS OF CALM." ALSO "POWELL'S BOOKS, SPENT HALF A DAY THERE."
OH, AND HITCHING IS ILLEGAL, "ALMOST GOT ARRESTED ON THE 101 TO ASTORIA BUT PLEADED IGNORANT TOURISTS."
THAT'S PRETTY SMART.
IF YOU SAY SO.
THIS ONE.
ON THE ROAD
SOMEONE HAS EXAMINED THE ORIGINAL MANUSCRIPT. YOU KNOW KEROUAC TAPED HIS PAPER TOGETHER SO HE WOULDN'T BREAK THE FLOW WHILE TYPING?
NO, BUT CARRY ON.
THEY'VE MARKED IN THE BOOK WHERE ONE TYPED PAGE OF THE ORIGINAL ENDED AND THE NEXT ONE STARTED.

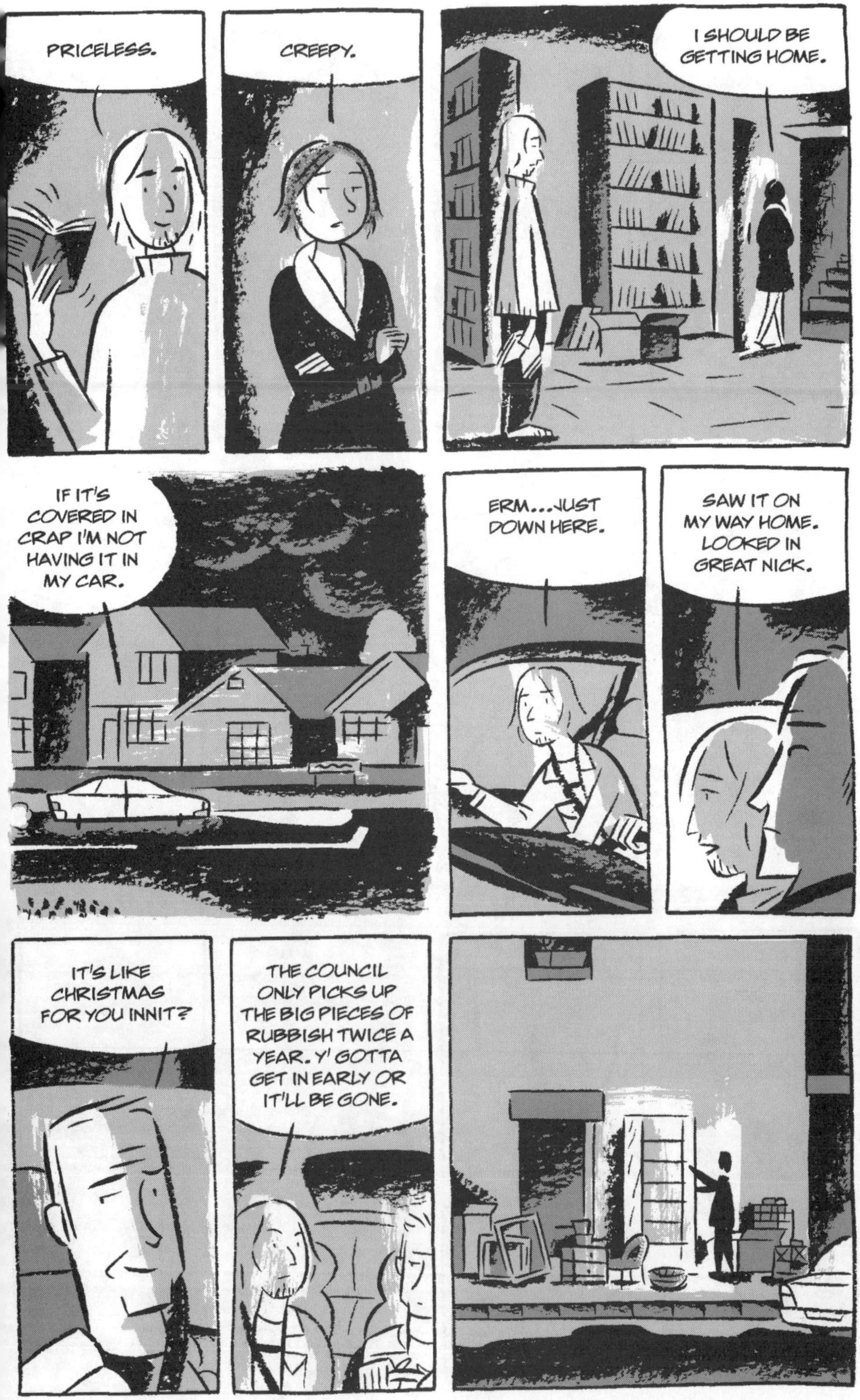
PRICELESS.
CREEPY.
I SHOULD BE GETTING HOME.
IF IT'S COVERED IN CRAP I'M NOT HAVING IT IN MY CAR.
ERM...JUST DOWN HERE.
SAW IT ON MY WAY HOME. LOOKED IN GREAT NICK.
IT'S LIKE CHRISTMAS FOR YOU INNIT?
THE COUNCIL ONLY PICKS UP THE BIG PIECES OF RUBBISH TWICE A YEAR. Y' GOTTA GET IN EARLY OR IT'LL BE GONE.

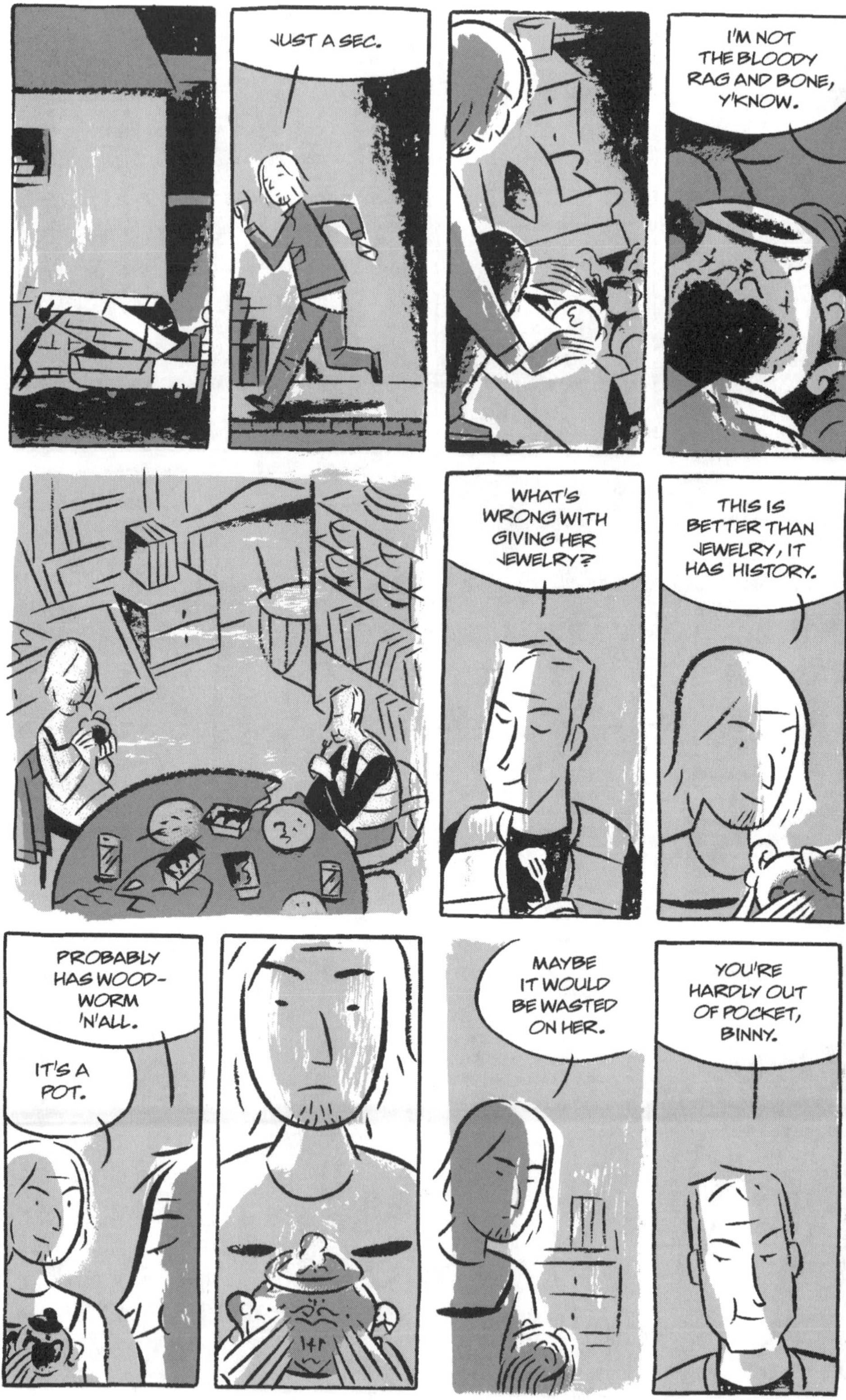
JUST A SEC.
I'M NOT THE BLOODY RAG AND BONE, Y'KNOW.
WHAT'S WRONG WITH GIVING HER JEWELRY?
THIS IS BETTER THAN JEWELRY, IT HAS HISTORY.
PROBABLY HAS WOOD-WORM 'N'ALL.
IT'S A POT.
MAYBE IT WOULD BE WASTED ON HER.
YOU'RE HARDLY OUT OF POCKET, BINNY.

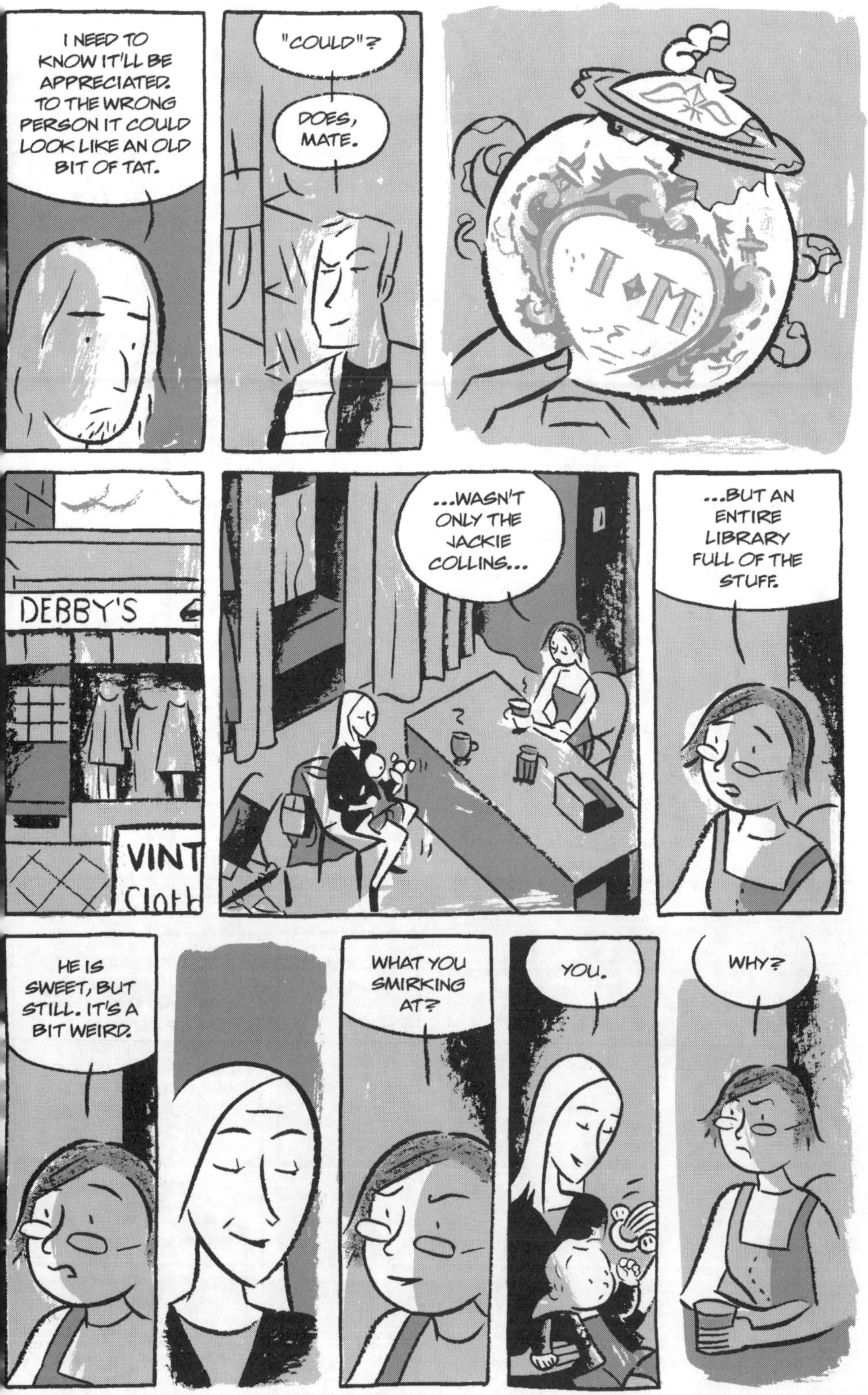
I NEED TO KNOW IT'LL BE APPRECIATED. TO THE WRONG PERSON IT COULD LOOK LIKE AN OLD BIT OF TAT.
"COULD"?
DOES, MATE.
I • M
DEBBY'S
VINT
Cloth
...WASN'T ONLY THE JACKIE COLLINS...
...BUT AN ENTIRE LIBRARY FULL OF THE STUFF.
HE IS SWEET, BUT STILL. IT'S A BIT WEIRD.
WHAT YOU SMIRKING AT?
YOU.
WHY?

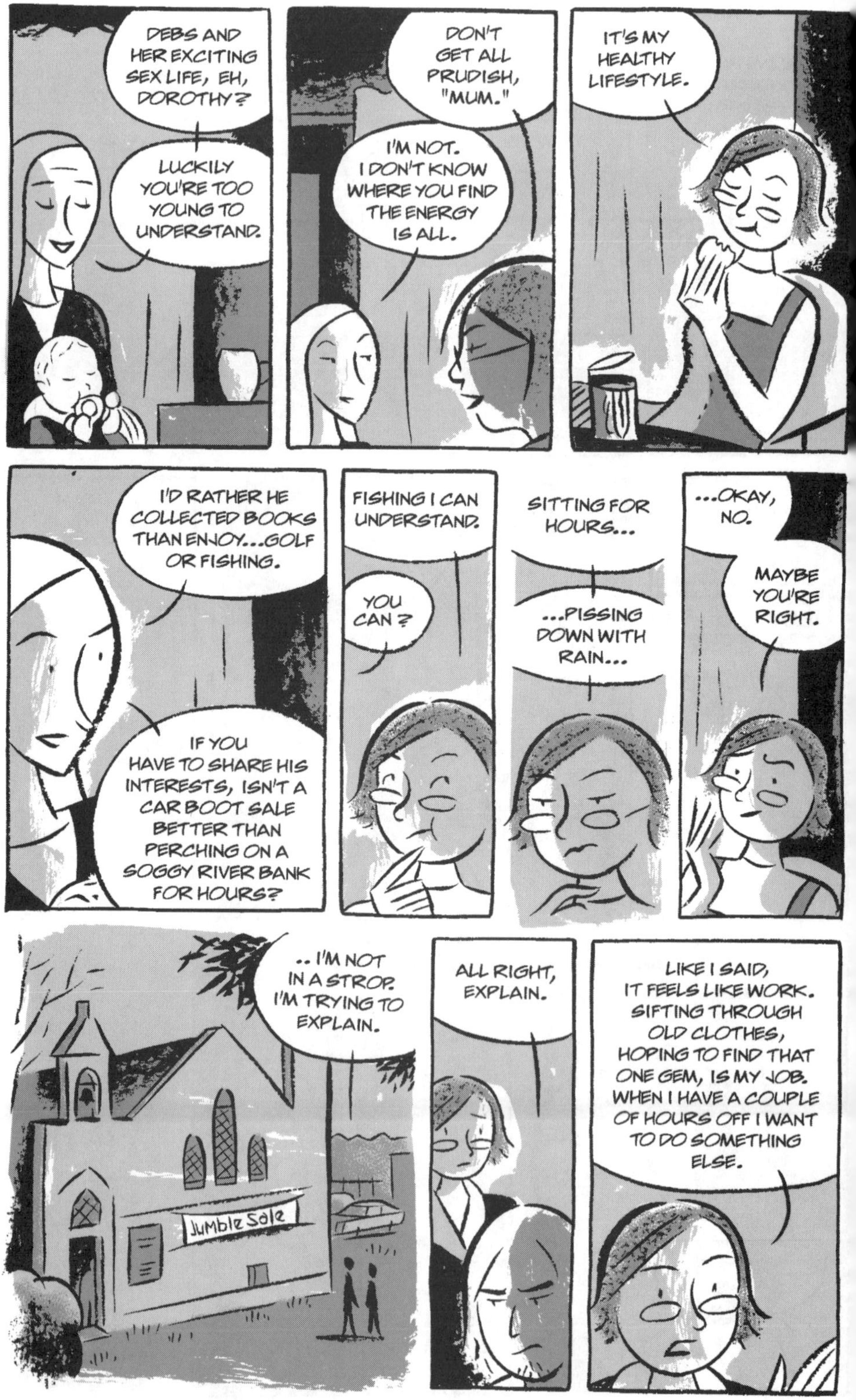
DEBS AND HER EXCITING SEX LIFE, EH, DOROTHY?
LUCKILY YOU'RE TOO YOUNG TO UNDERSTAND.
DON'T GET ALL PRUDISH, "MUM."
I'M NOT. I DON'T KNOW WHERE YOU FIND THE ENERGY IS ALL.
IT'S MY HEALTHY LIFESTYLE.
I'D RATHER HE COLLECTED BOOKS THAN ENJOY...GOLF OR FISHING.
IF YOU HAVE TO SHARE HIS INTERESTS, ISN'T A CAR BOOT SALE BETTER THAN PERCHING ON A SOGGY RIVER BANK FOR HOURS?
FISHING I CAN UNDERSTAND.
YOU CAN?
SITTING FOR HOURS...
...PISSING DOWN WITH RAIN...
...OKAY, NO.
MAYBE YOU'RE RIGHT.
Jumble Sale
.. I'M NOT IN A STROP. I'M TRYING TO EXPLAIN.
ALL RIGHT, EXPLAIN.
LIKE I SAID, IT FEELS LIKE WORK. SIFTING THROUGH OLD CLOTHES, HOPING TO FIND THAT ONE GEM, IS MY JOB. WHEN I HAVE A COUPLE OF HOURS OFF I WANT TO DO SOMETHING ELSE.

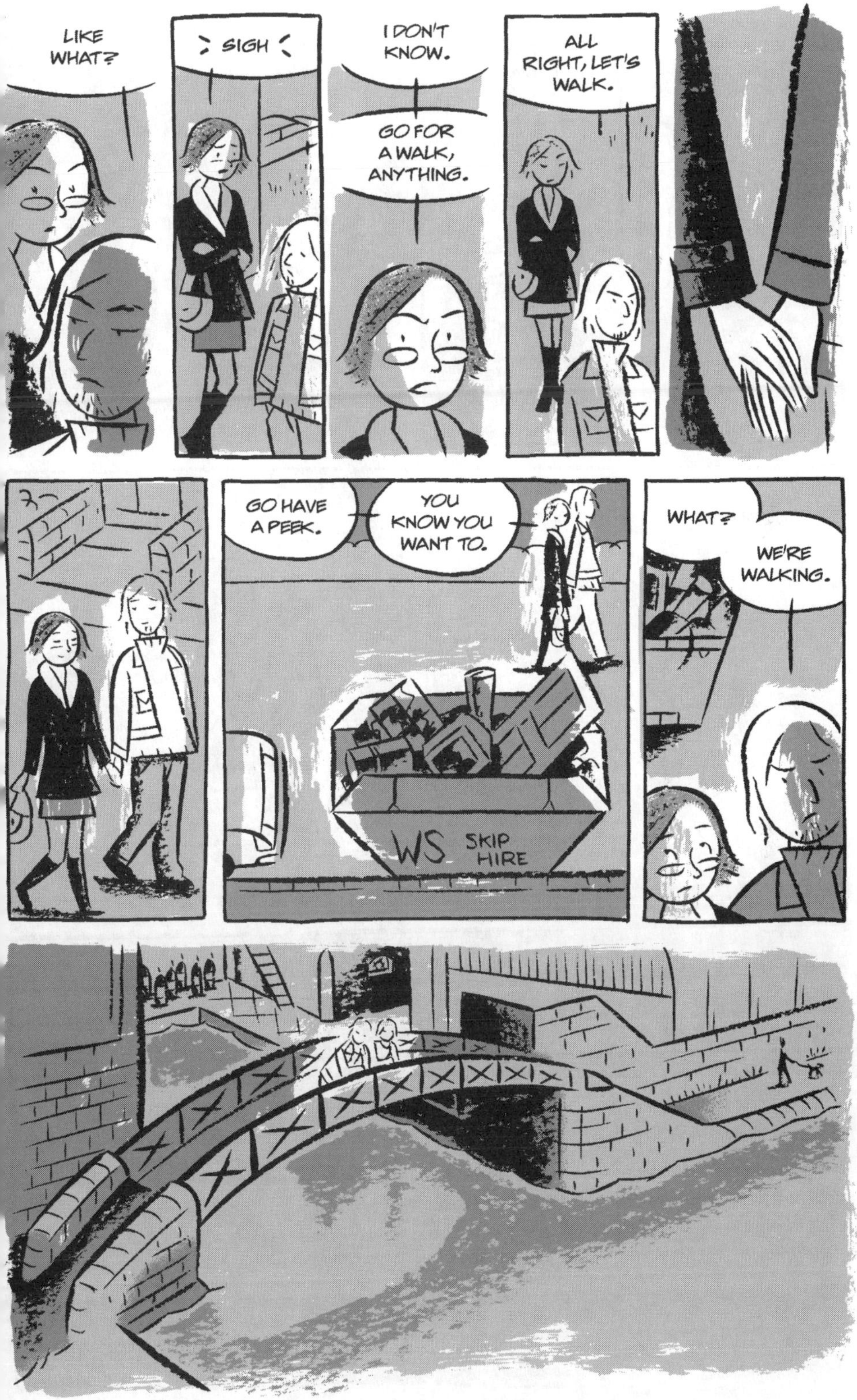
LIKE WHAT?
SIGH
I DON'T KNOW.
GO FOR A WALK, ANYTHING.
ALL RIGHT, LET'S WALK.
GO HAVE A PEEK.
YOU KNOW YOU WANT TO.
WS SKIP HIRE
WHAT?
WE'RE WALKING.

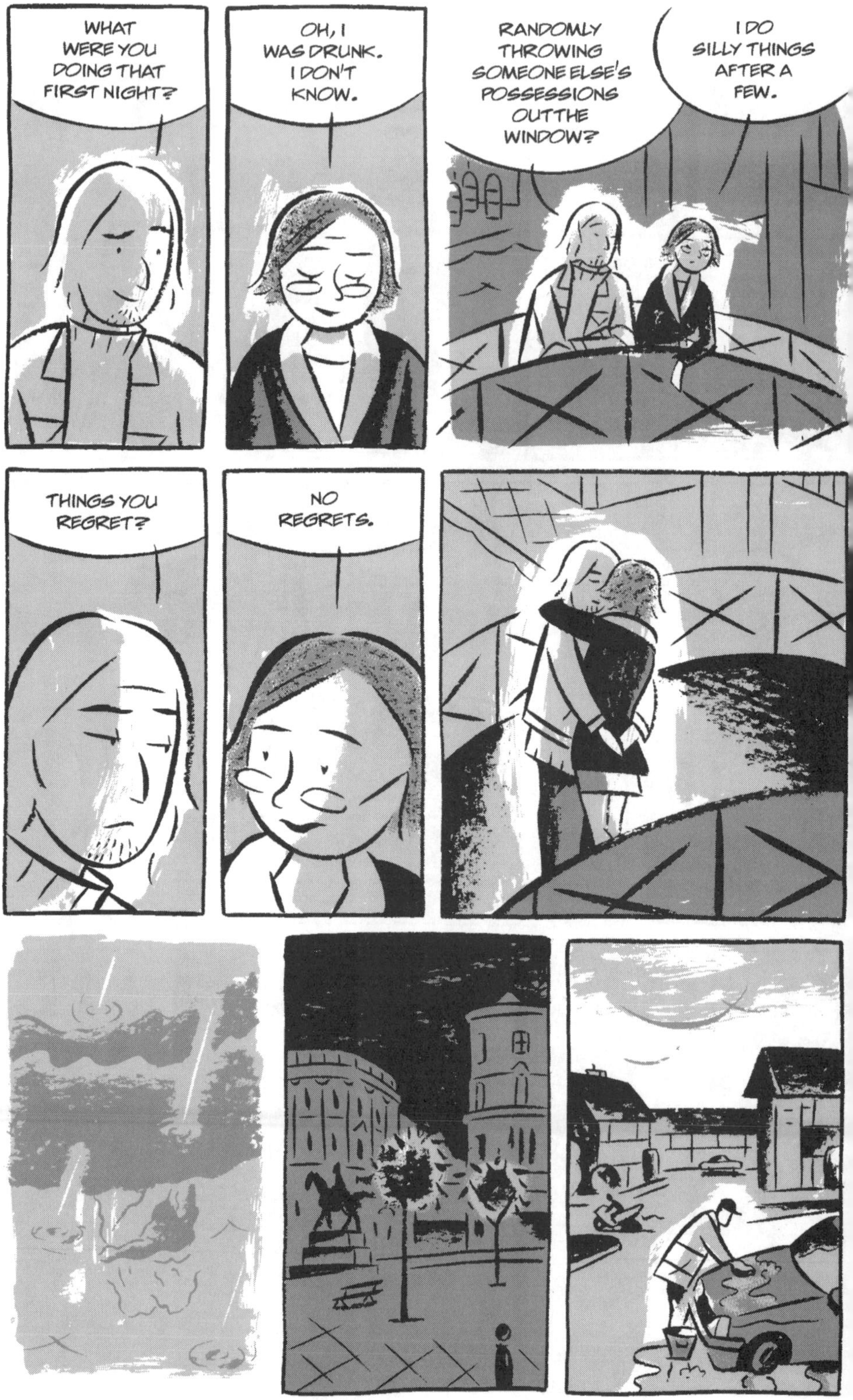
WHAT WERE YOU DOING THAT FIRST NIGHT?
OH, I WAS DRUNK. I DON'T KNOW.
RANDOMLY THROWING SOMEONE ELSE'S POSSESSIONS OUT THE WINDOW?
I DO SILLY THINGS AFTER A FEW.
THINGS YOU REGRET?
NO REGRETS.

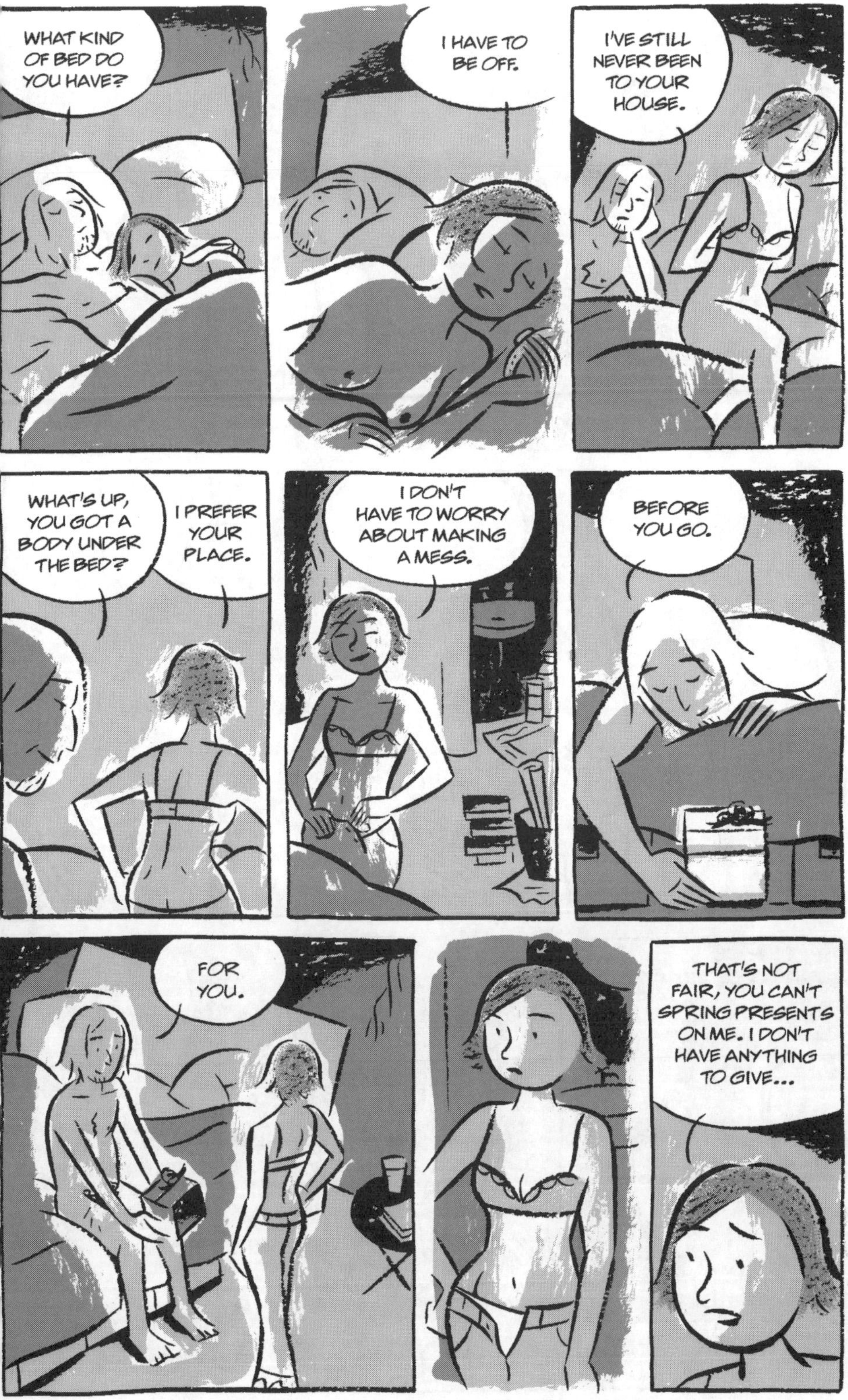
WHAT KIND OF BED DO YOU HAVE?
I HAVE TO BE OFF.
I'VE STILL NEVER BEEN TO YOUR HOUSE.
WHAT'S UP, YOU GOT A BODY UNDER THE BED?
I PREFER YOUR PLACE.
I DON'T HAVE TO WORRY ABOUT MAKING A MESS.
BEFORE YOU GO.
FOR YOU.
THAT'S NOT FAIR, YOU CAN'T SPRING PRESENTS ON ME. I DON'T HAVE ANYTHING TO GIVE...

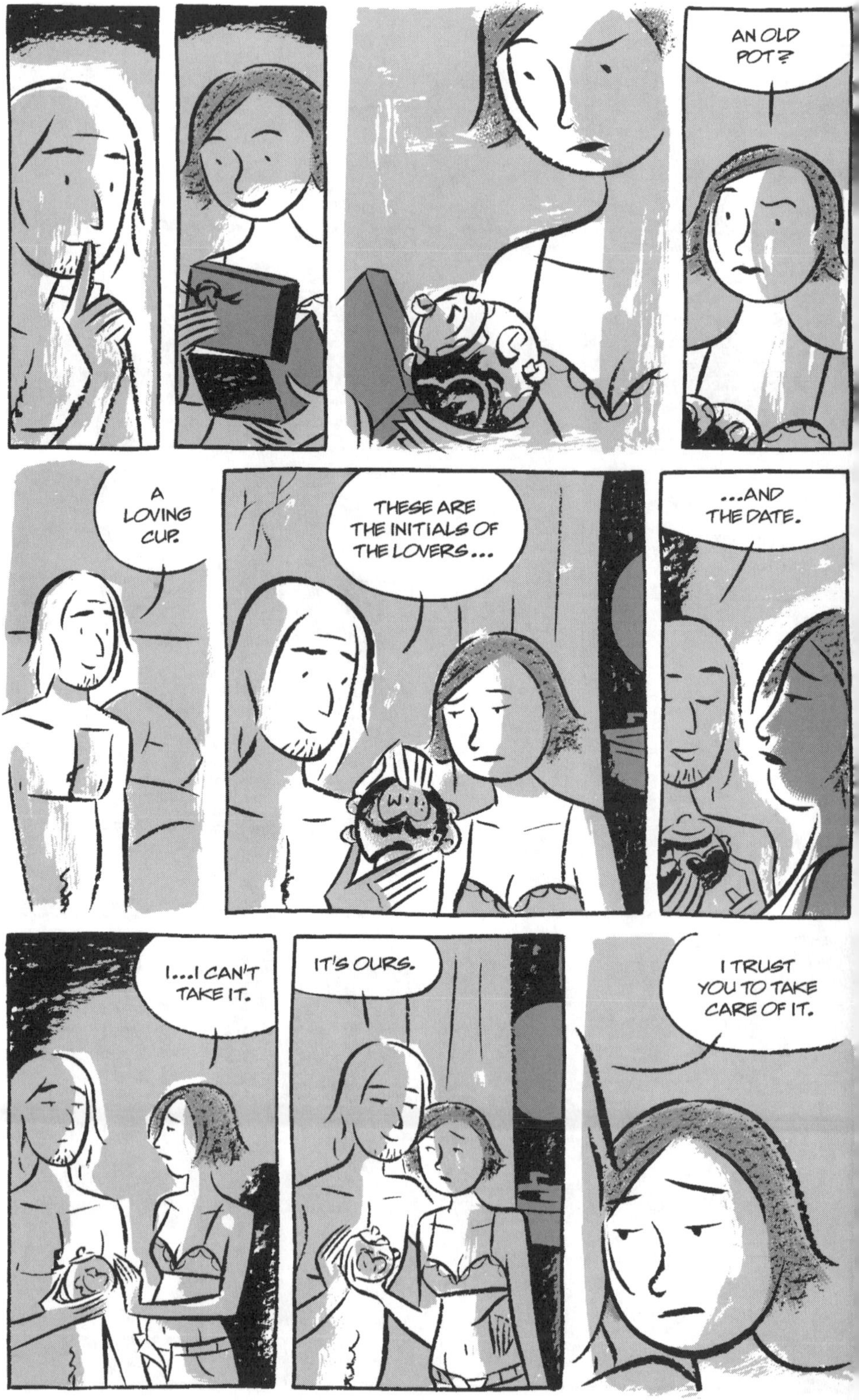
AN OLD POT?
A LOVING CUP.
THESE ARE THE INITIALS OF THE LOVERS...
...AND THE DATE.
I...I CAN'T TAKE IT.
IT'S OURS.
I TRUST YOU TO TAKE CARE OF IT.

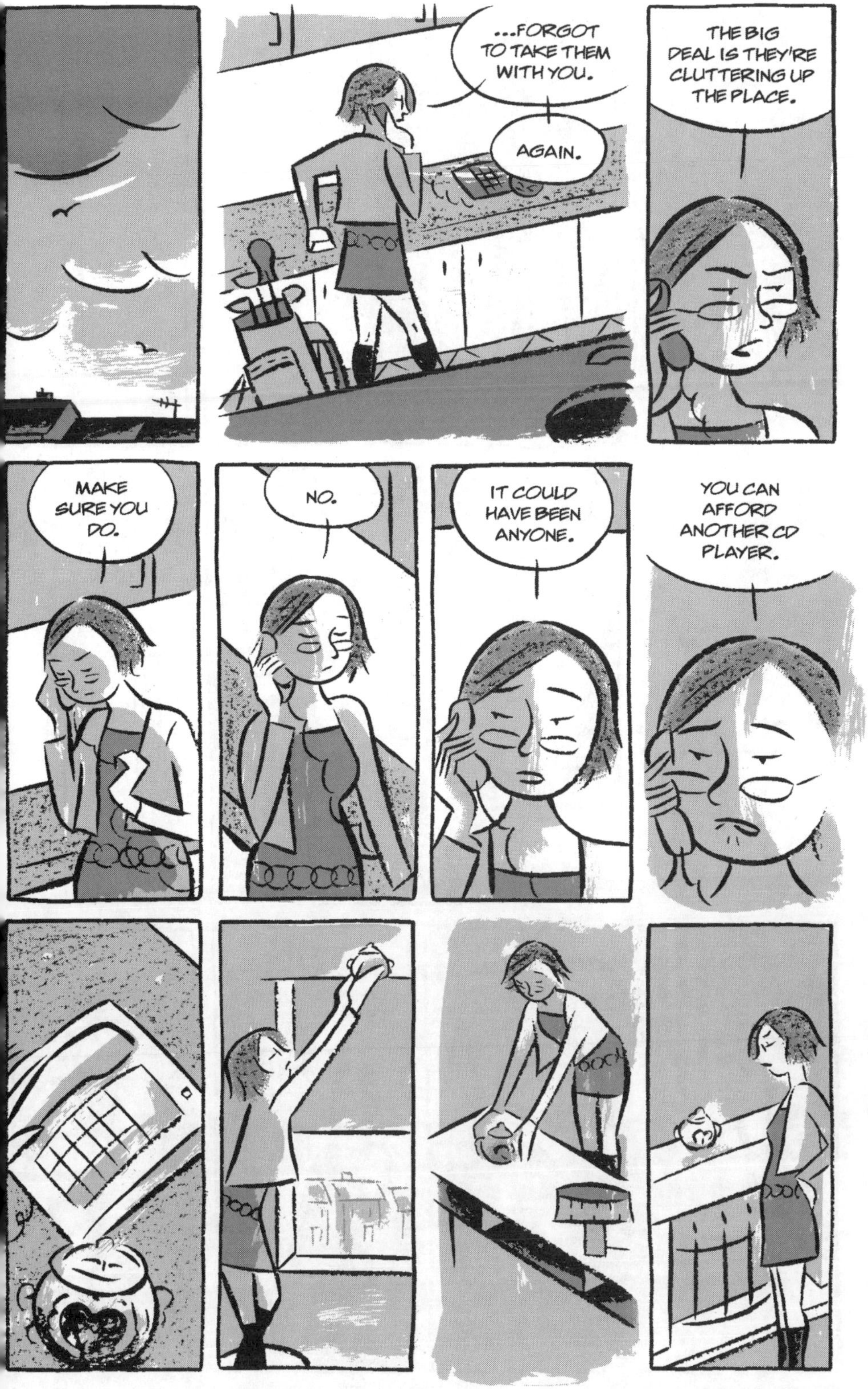
...FORGOT TO TAKE THEM WITH YOU.
AGAIN.
THE BIG DEAL IS THEY'RE CLUTTERING UP THE PLACE.
MAKE SURE YOU DO.
NO.
IT COULD HAVE BEEN ANYONE.
YOU CAN AFFORD ANOTHER CD PLAYER.

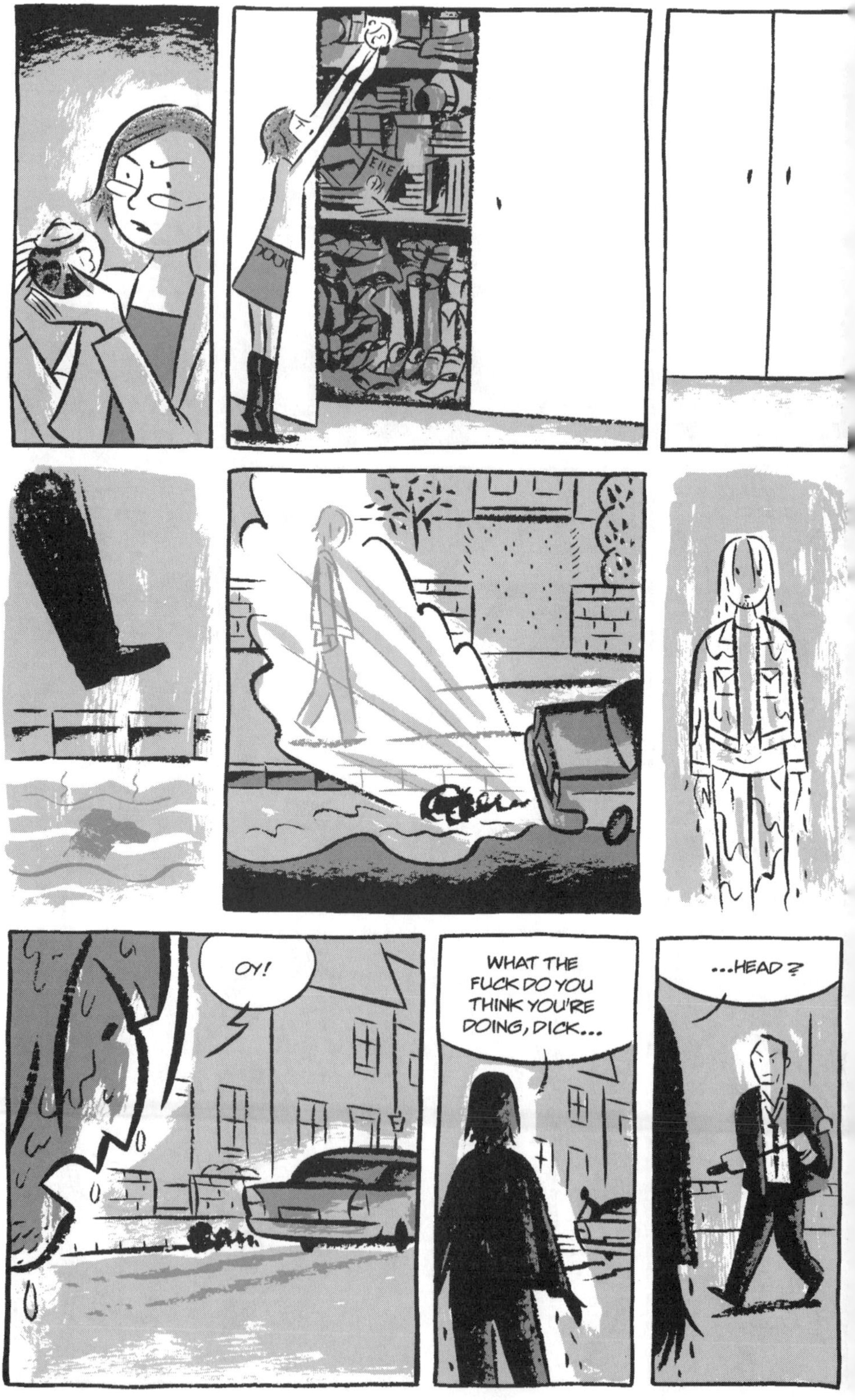
OY!
WHAT THE FUCK DO YOU THINK YOU'RE DOING, DICK...
...HEAD ?

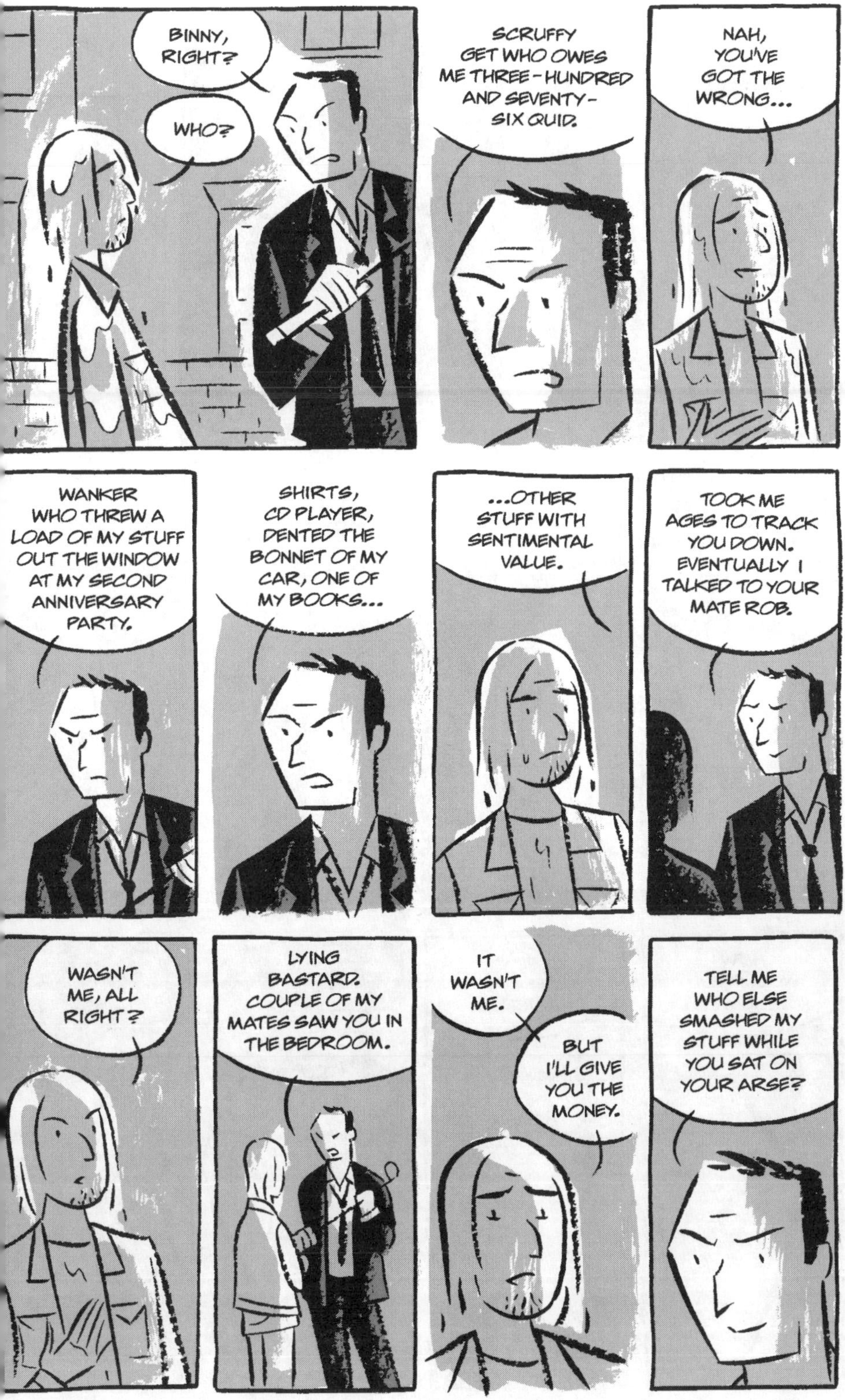
BINNY, RIGHT?
WHO?
SCRUFFY GET WHO OWES ME THREE-HUNDRED AND SEVENTY-SIX QUID.
NAH, YOU'VE GOT THE WRONG...
WANKER WHO THREW A LOAD OF MY STUFF OUT THE WINDOW AT MY SECOND ANNIVERSARY PARTY.
SHIRTS, CD PLAYER, DENTED THE BONNET OF MY CAR, ONE OF MY BOOKS...
...OTHER STUFF WITH SENTIMENTAL VALUE.
TOOK ME AGES TO TRACK YOU DOWN. EVENTUALLY I TALKED TO YOUR MATE ROB.
WASN'T ME, ALL RIGHT?
LYING BASTARD. COUPLE OF MY MATES SAW YOU IN THE BEDROOM.
IT WASN'T ME.
BUT I'LL GIVE YOU THE MONEY.
TELL ME WHO ELSE SMASHED MY STUFF WHILE YOU SAT ON YOUR ARSE?

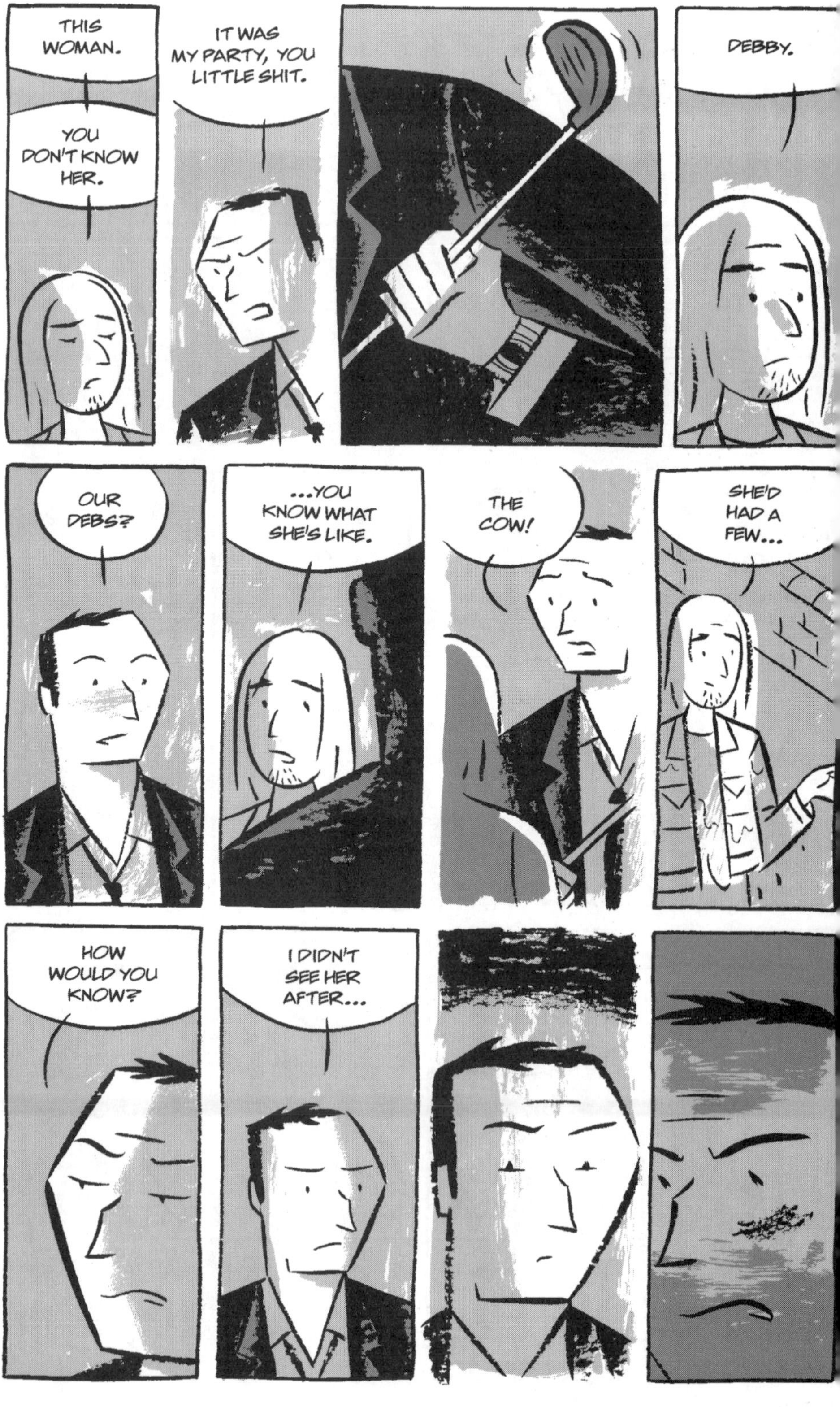
THIS WOMAN.
YOU DON'T KNOW HER.
IT WAS MY PARTY, YOU LITTLE SHIT.
DEBBY.
OUR DEBS?
...YOU KNOW WHAT SHE'S LIKE.
THE COW!
SHE'D HAD A FEW...
HOW WOULD YOU KNOW?
I DIDN'T SEE HER AFTER...

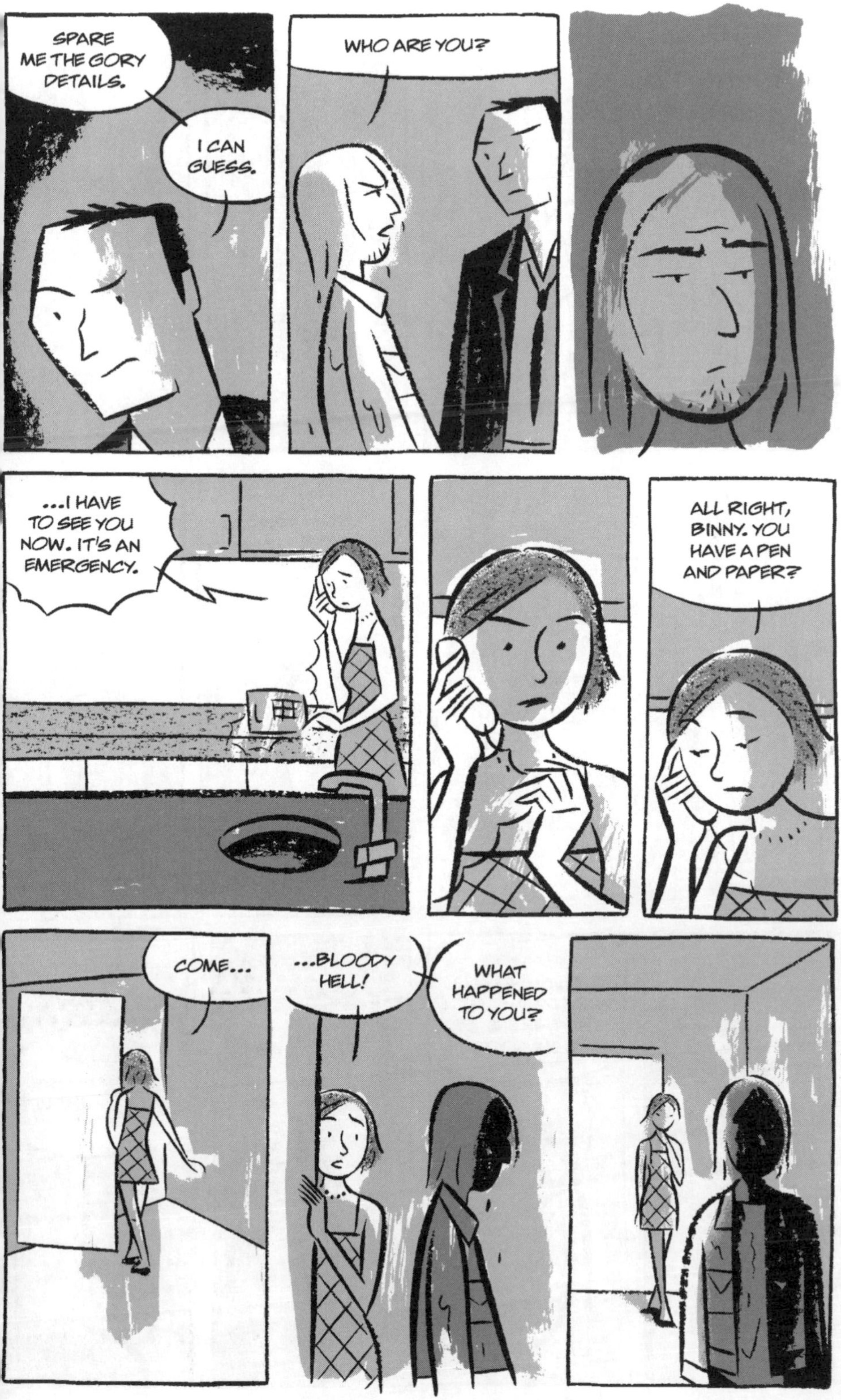
SPARE ME THE GORY DETAILS.
I CAN GUESS.
WHO ARE YOU?
...I HAVE TO SEE YOU NOW. IT'S AN EMERGENCY.
ALL RIGHT, BINNY. YOU HAVE A PEN AND PAPER?
COME...
...BLOODY HELL!
WHAT HAPPENED TO YOU?

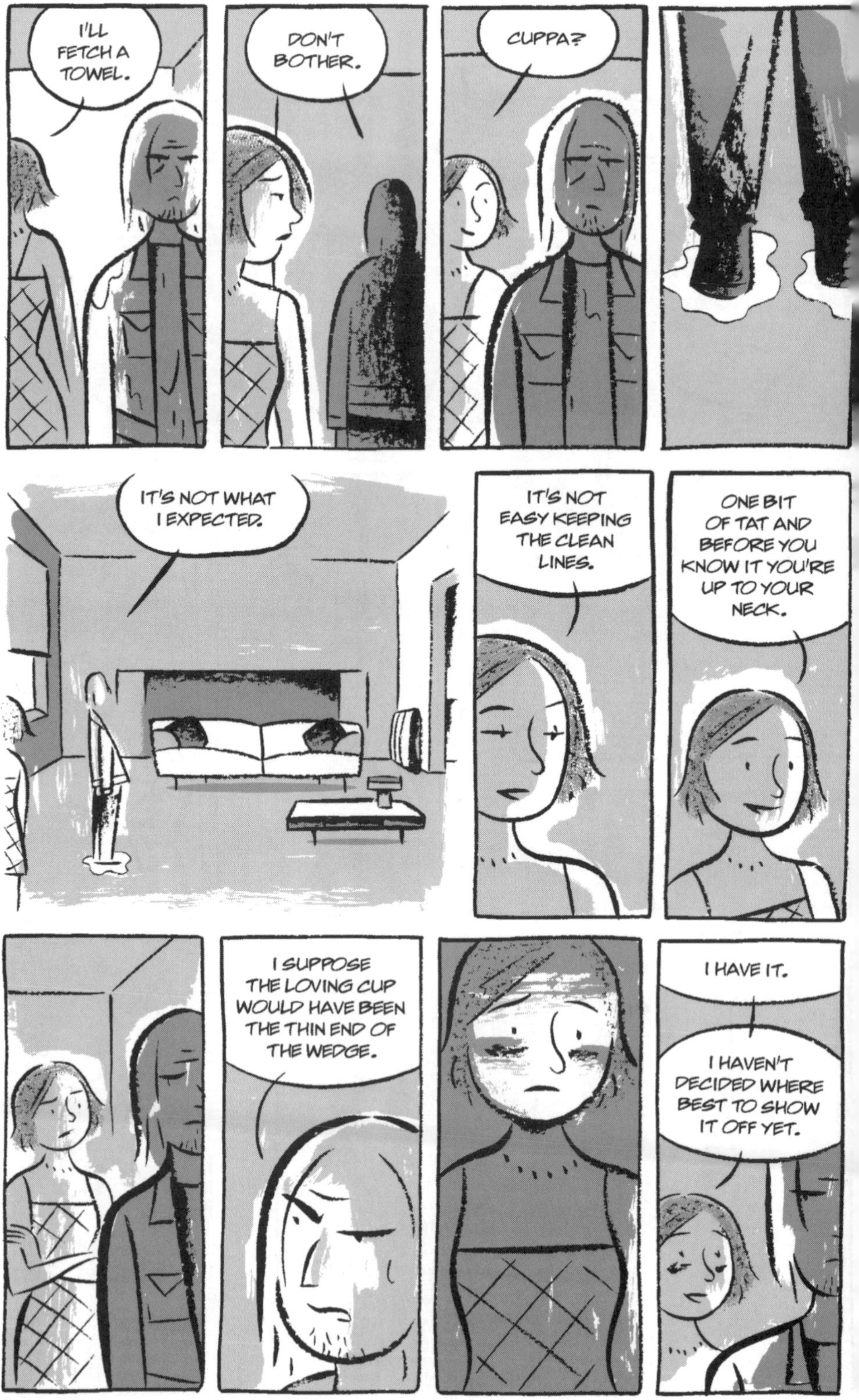
I'LL FETCH A TOWEL.
DON'T BOTHER.
CUPPA?
IT'S NOT WHAT I EXPECTED.
IT'S NOT EASY KEEPING THE CLEAN LINES.
ONE BIT OF TAT AND BEFORE YOU KNOW IT YOU'RE UP TO YOUR NECK.
I SUPPOSE THE LOVING CUP WOULD HAVE BEEN THE THIN END OF THE WEDGE.
I HAVE IT.
I HAVEN'T DECIDED WHERE BEST TO SHOW IT OFF YET.

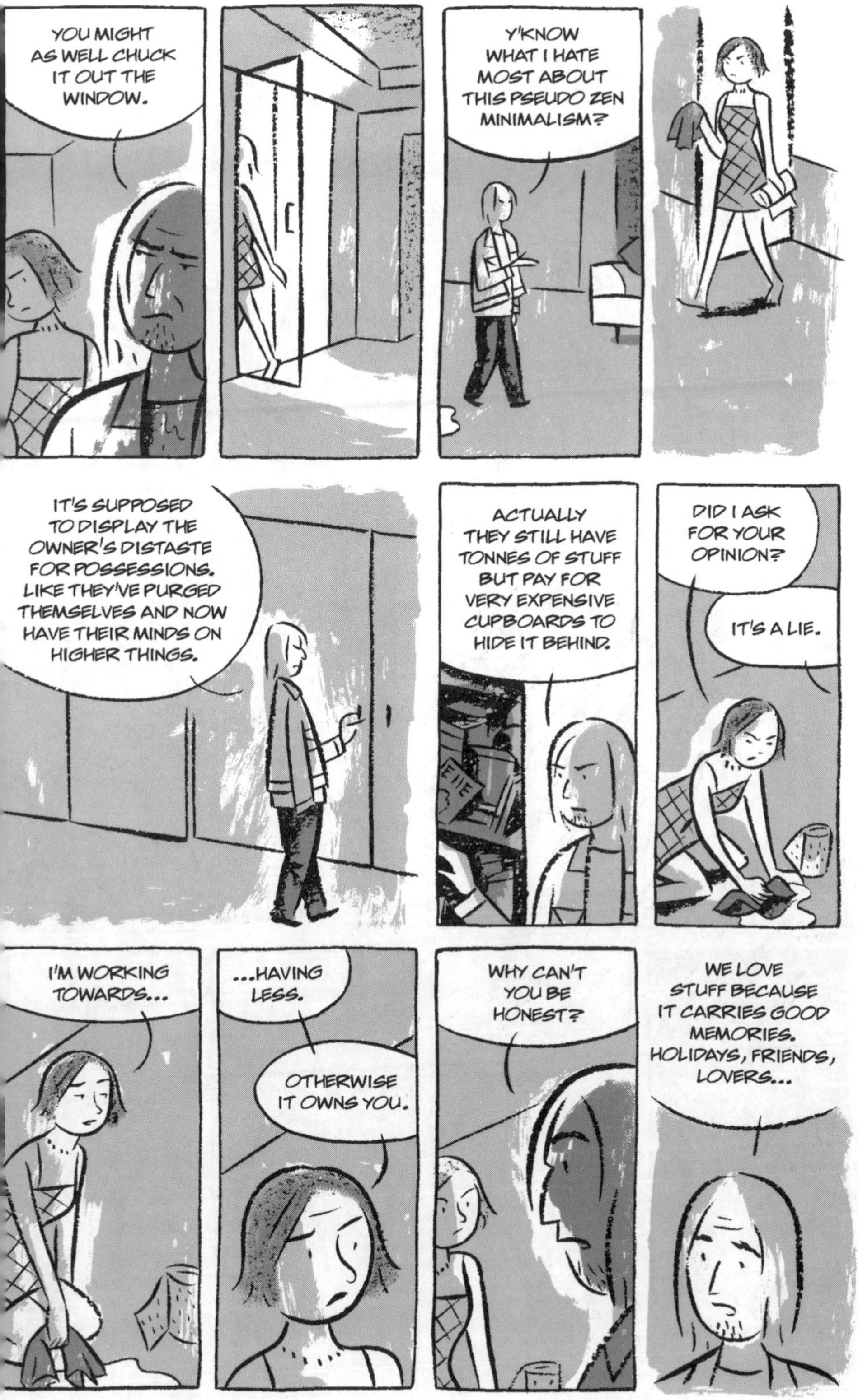
YOU MIGHT AS WELL CHUCK IT OUT THE WINDOW.
Y'KNOW WHAT I HATE MOST ABOUT THIS PSEUDO ZEN MINIMALISM?
IT'S SUPPOSED TO DISPLAY THE OWNER'S DISTASTE FOR POSSESSIONS. LIKE THEY'VE PURGED THEMSELVES AND NOW HAVE THEIR MINDS ON HIGHER THINGS.
ACTUALLY THEY STILL HAVE TONNES OF STUFF BUT PAY FOR VERY EXPENSIVE CUPBOARDS TO HIDE IT BEHIND.
DID I ASK FOR YOUR OPINION?
IT'S A LIE.
I'M WORKING TOWARDS...
...HAVING LESS.
OTHERWISE IT OWNS YOU.
WHY CAN'T YOU BE HONEST?
WE LOVE STUFF BECAUSE IT CARRIES GOOD MEMORIES. HOLIDAYS, FRIENDS, LOVERS...

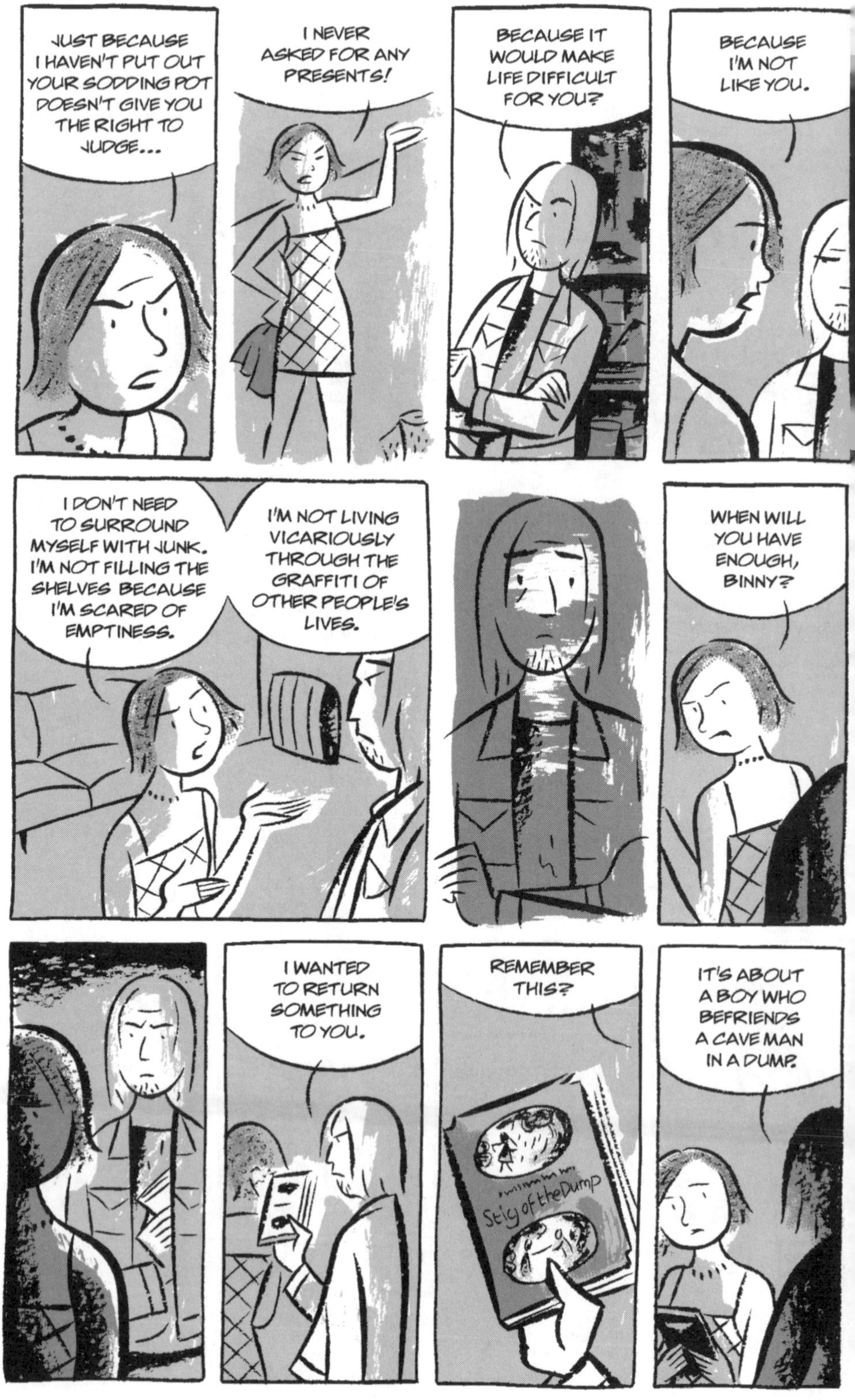
JUST BECAUSE I HAVEN'T PUT OUT YOUR SODDING POT DOESN'T GIVE YOU THE RIGHT TO JUDGE...
I NEVER ASKED FOR ANY PRESENTS!
BECAUSE IT WOULD MAKE LIFE DIFFICULT FOR YOU?
BECAUSE I'M NOT LIKE YOU.
I DON'T NEED TO SURROUND MYSELF WITH JUNK. I'M NOT FILLING THE SHELVES BECAUSE I'M SCARED OF EMPTINESS.
I'M NOT LIVING VICARIOUSLY THROUGH THE GRAFFITI OF OTHER PEOPLE'S LIVES.
WHEN WILL YOU HAVE ENOUGH, BINNY?
I WANTED TO RETURN SOMETHING TO YOU.
REMEMBER THIS?
Stig of the Dump
IT'S ABOUT A BOY WHO BEFRIENDS A CAVE MAN IN A DUMP.

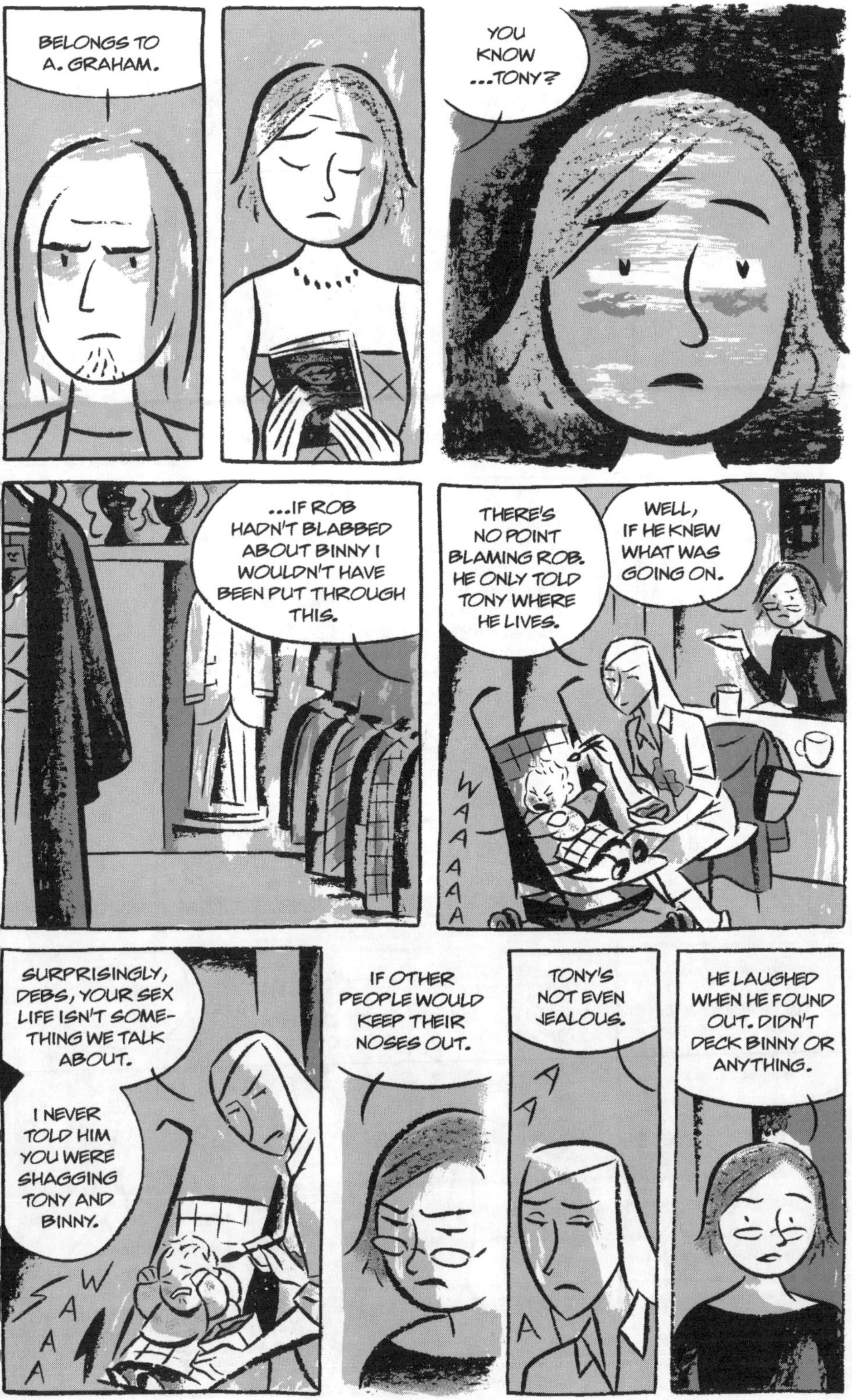

BELONGS TO A. GRAHAM.
YOU KNOW ...TONY?
...IF ROB HADN'T BLABBED ABOUT BINNY I WOULDN'T HAVE BEEN PUT THROUGH THIS.
THERE'S NO POINT BLAMING ROB. HE ONLY TOLD TONY WHERE HE LIVES.
WELL, IF HE KNEW WHAT WAS GOING ON.
WAAAAAA
SURPRISINGLY, DEBS, YOUR SEX LIFE ISN'T SOME-THING WE TALK ABOUT.
I NEVER TOLD HIM YOU WERE SHAGGING TONY AND BINNY.
WAAAA
IF OTHER PEOPLE WOULD KEEP THEIR NOSES OUT.
TONY'S NOT EVEN JEALOUS.
AAA
HE LAUGHED WHEN HE FOUND OUT. DIDN'T DECK BINNY OR ANYTHING.

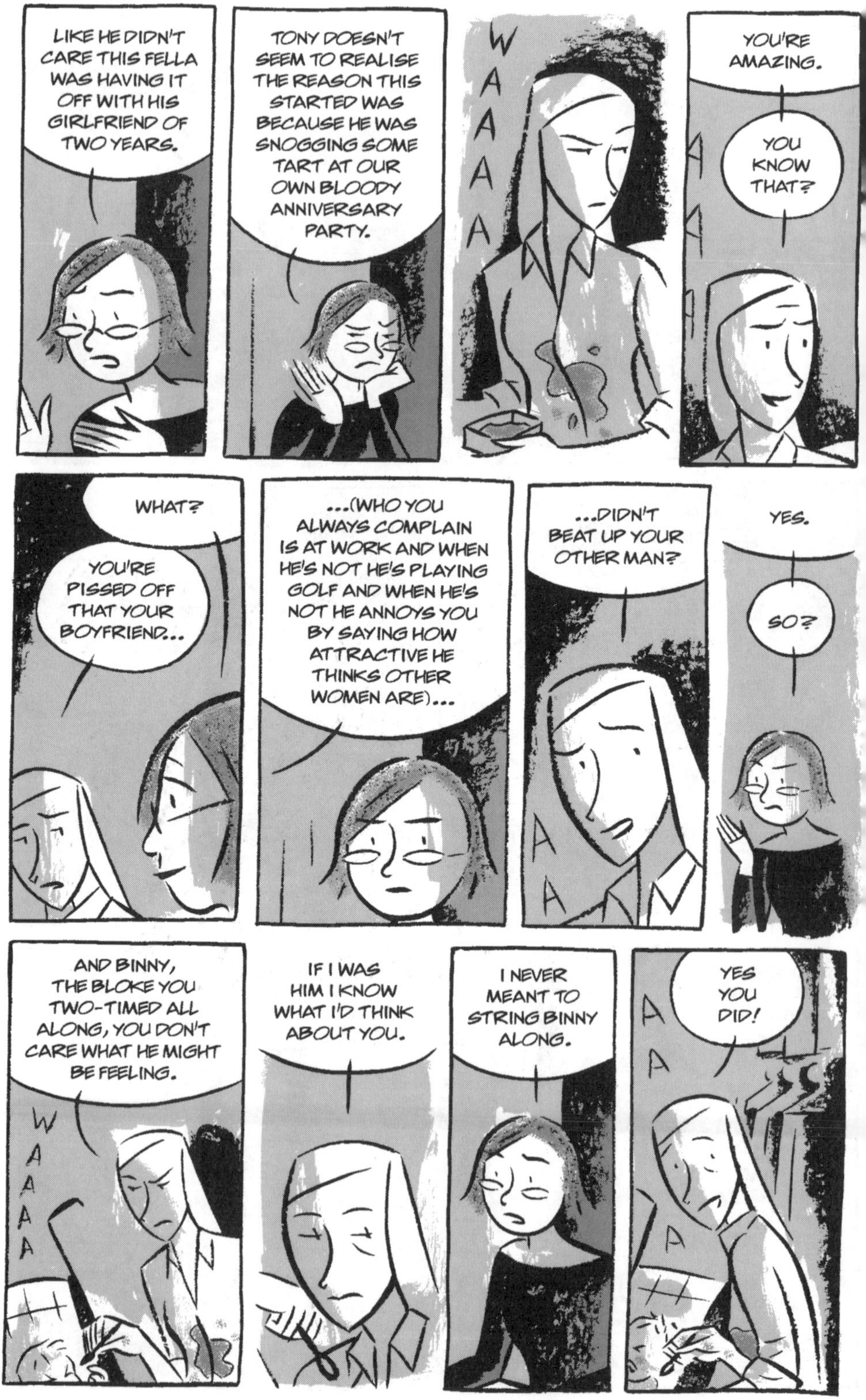

LIKE HE DIDN'T CARE THIS FELLA WAS HAVING IT OFF WITH HIS GIRLFRIEND OF TWO YEARS.
TONY DOESN'T SEEM TO REALISE THE REASON THIS STARTED WAS BECAUSE HE WAS SNOGGING SOME TART AT OUR OWN BLOODY ANNIVERSARY PARTY.
WAAAAA
YOU'RE AMAZING.
YOU KNOW THAT?
AAA
WHAT?
YOU'RE PISSED OFF THAT YOUR BOYFRIEND...
...(WHO YOU ALWAYS COMPLAIN IS AT WORK AND WHEN HE'S NOT HE'S PLAYING GOLF AND WHEN HE'S NOT HE ANNOYS YOU BY SAYING HOW ATTRACTIVE HE THINKS OTHER WOMEN ARE)...
...DIDN'T BEAT UP YOUR OTHER MAN?
AA
YES.
SO?
AND BINNY, THE BLOKE YOU TWO-TIMED ALL ALONG, YOU DON'T CARE WHAT HE MIGHT BE FEELING.
WAAAAA
IF I WAS HIM I KNOW WHAT I'D THINK ABOUT YOU.
I NEVER MEANT TO STRING BINNY ALONG.
YES YOU DID!
AAA

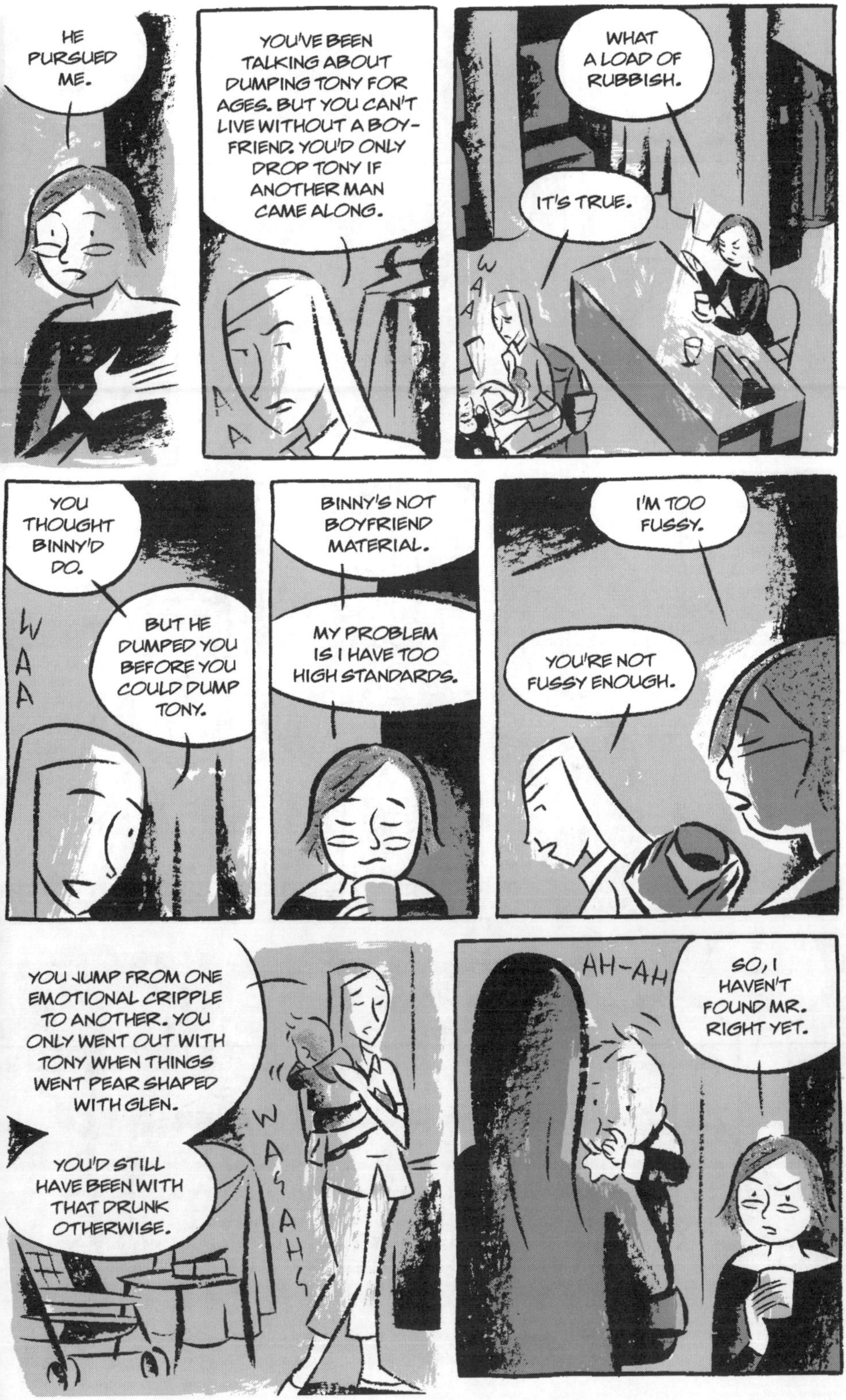

HE PURSUED ME.
YOU'VE BEEN TALKING ABOUT DUMPING TONY FOR AGES. BUT YOU CAN'T LIVE WITHOUT A BOY-FRIEND. YOU'D ONLY DROP TONY IF ANOTHER MAN CAME ALONG.
AA
WHAT A LOAD OF RUBBISH.
IT'S TRUE.
WAA
YOU THOUGHT BINNY'D DO.
BUT HE DUMPED YOU BEFORE YOU COULD DUMP TONY.
WAA
BINNY'S NOT BOYFRIEND MATERIAL.
MY PROBLEM IS I HAVE TOO HIGH STANDARDS.
I'M TOO FUSSY.
YOU'RE NOT FUSSY ENOUGH.
YOU JUMP FROM ONE EMOTIONAL CRIPPLE TO ANOTHER. YOU ONLY WENT OUT WITH TONY WHEN THINGS WENT PEAR SHAPED WITH GLEN.
YOU'D STILL HAVE BEEN WITH THAT DRUNK OTHERWISE.
WAAAHH
AH-AH
SO, I HAVEN'T FOUND MR. RIGHT YET.

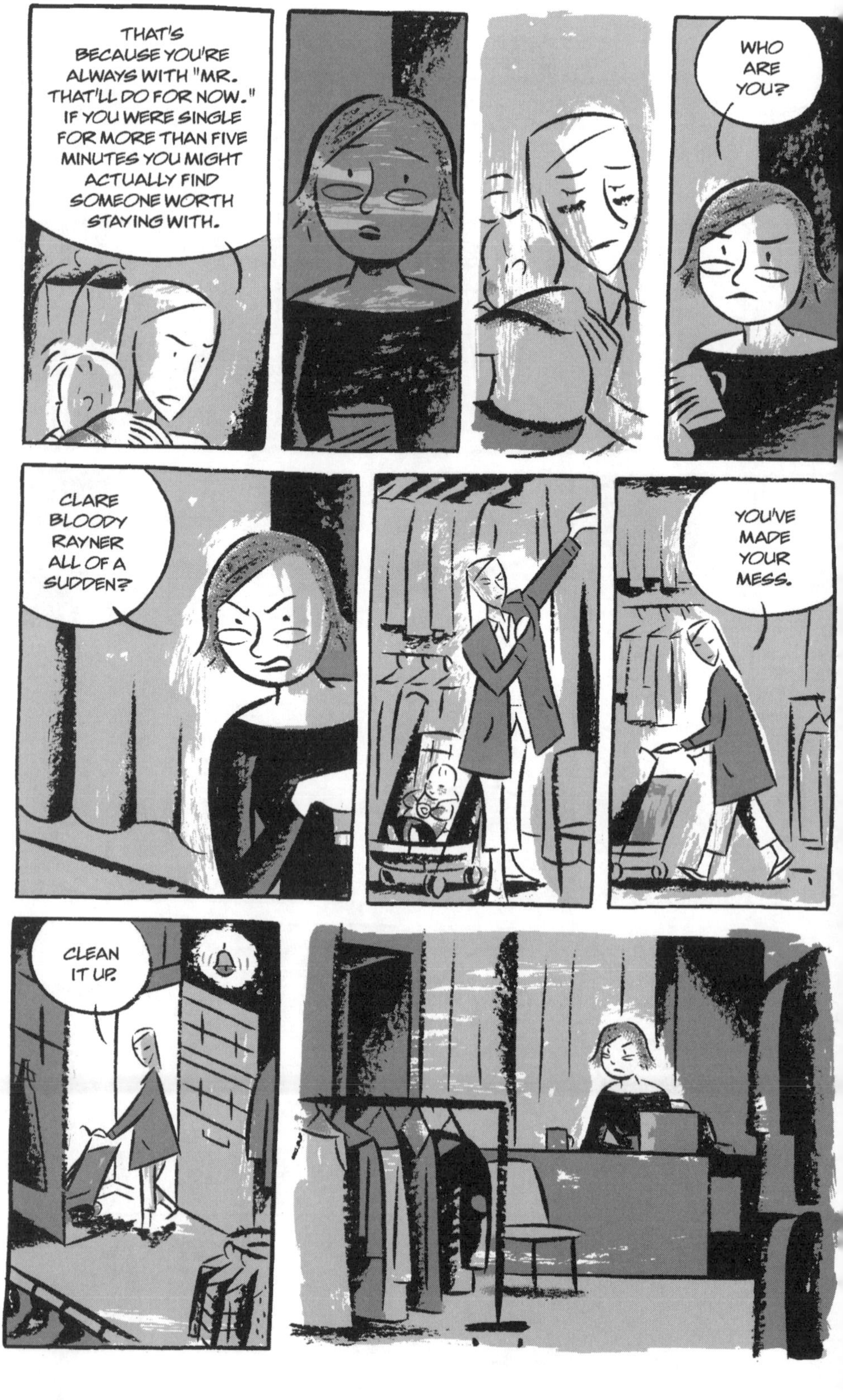

THAT'S BECAUSE YOU'RE ALWAYS WITH "MR. THAT'LL DO FOR NOW." IF YOU WERE SINGLE FOR MORE THAN FIVE MINUTES YOU MIGHT ACTUALLY FIND SOMEONE WORTH STAYING WITH.
WHO ARE YOU?
CLARE BLOODY RAYNER ALL OF A SUDDEN?
YOU'VE MADE YOUR MESS.
CLEAN IT UP.

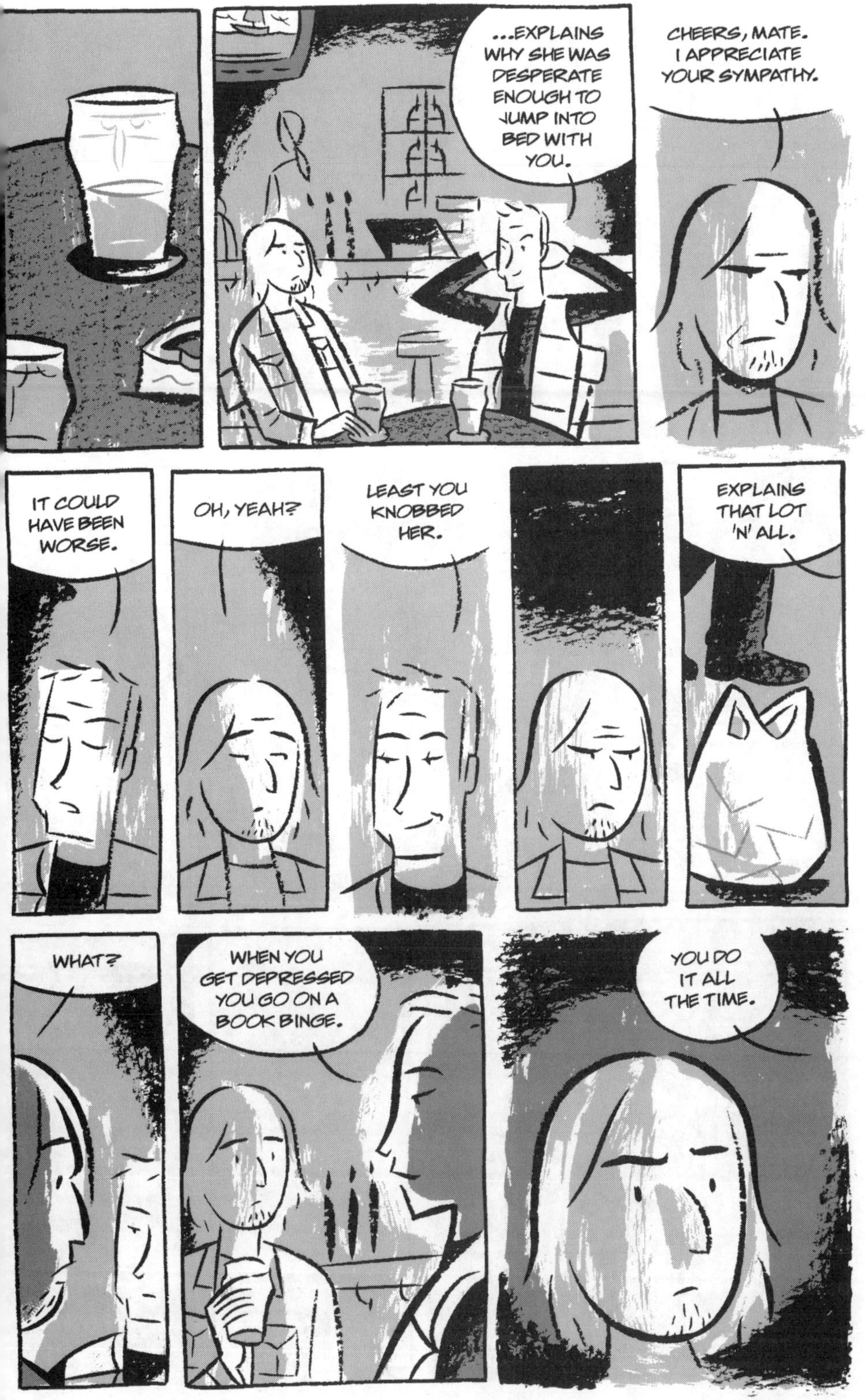
...EXPLAINS WHY SHE WAS DESPERATE ENOUGH TO JUMP INTO BED WITH YOU.
CHEERS, MATE. I APPRECIATE YOUR SYMPATHY.
IT COULD HAVE BEEN WORSE.
OH, YEAH?
LEAST YOU KNOBBED HER.
EXPLAINS THAT LOT 'N' ALL.
WHAT?
WHEN YOU GET DEPRESSED YOU GO ON A BOOK BINGE.
YOU DO IT ALL THE TIME.

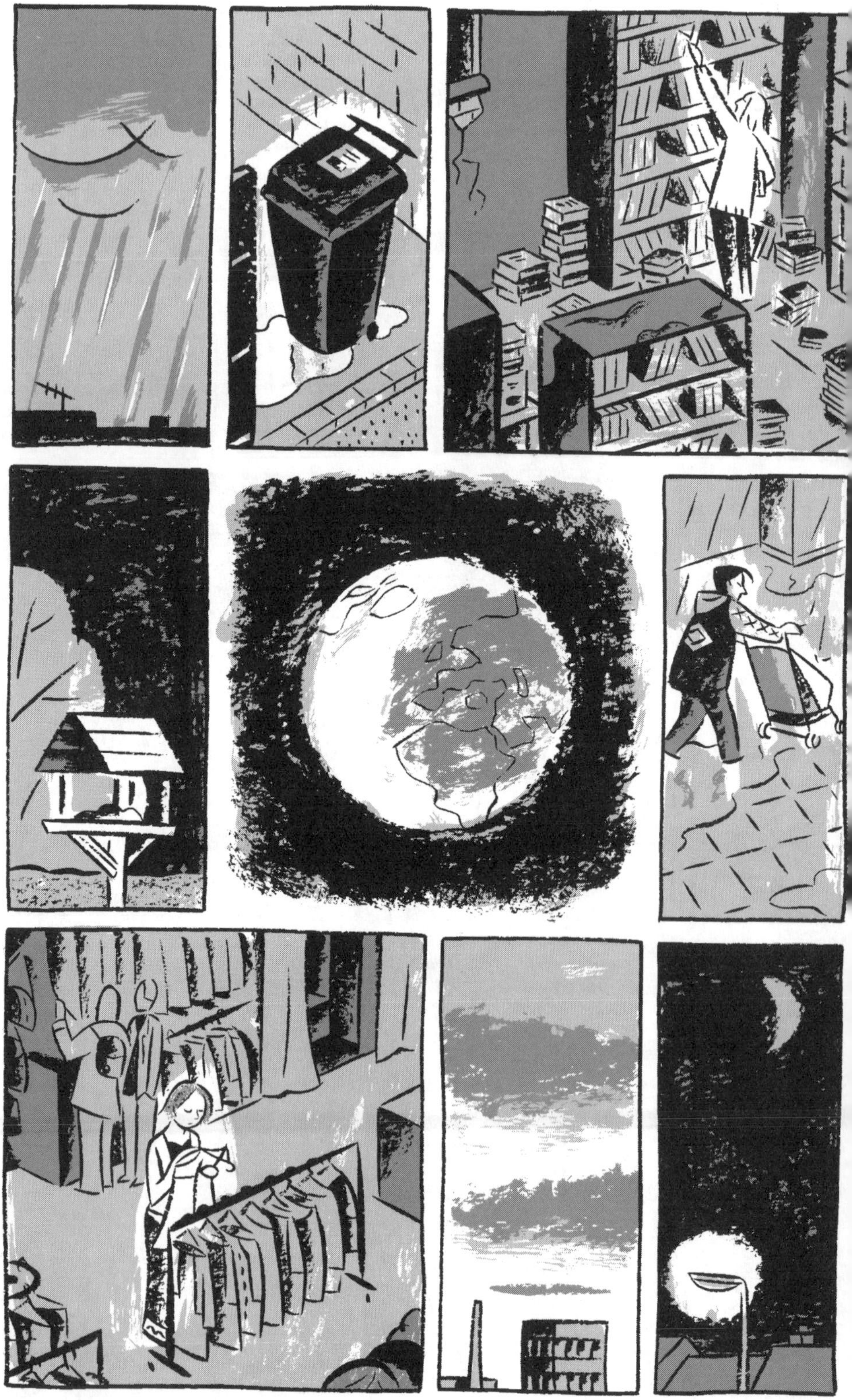

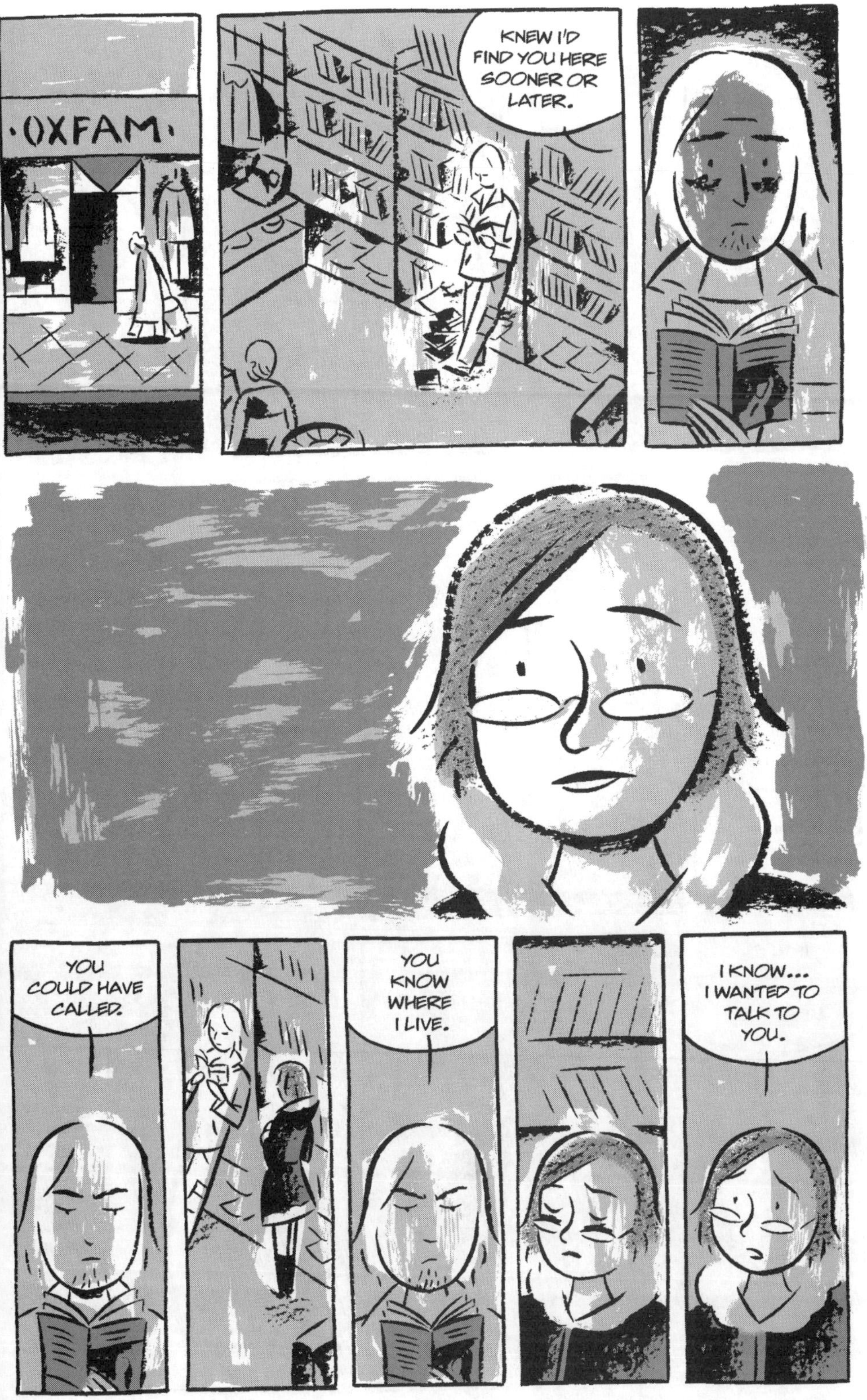
·OXFAM·
KNEW I'D FIND YOU HERE SOONER OR LATER.
YOU COULD HAVE CALLED.
YOU KNOW WHERE I LIVE.
I KNOW... I WANTED TO TALK TO YOU.

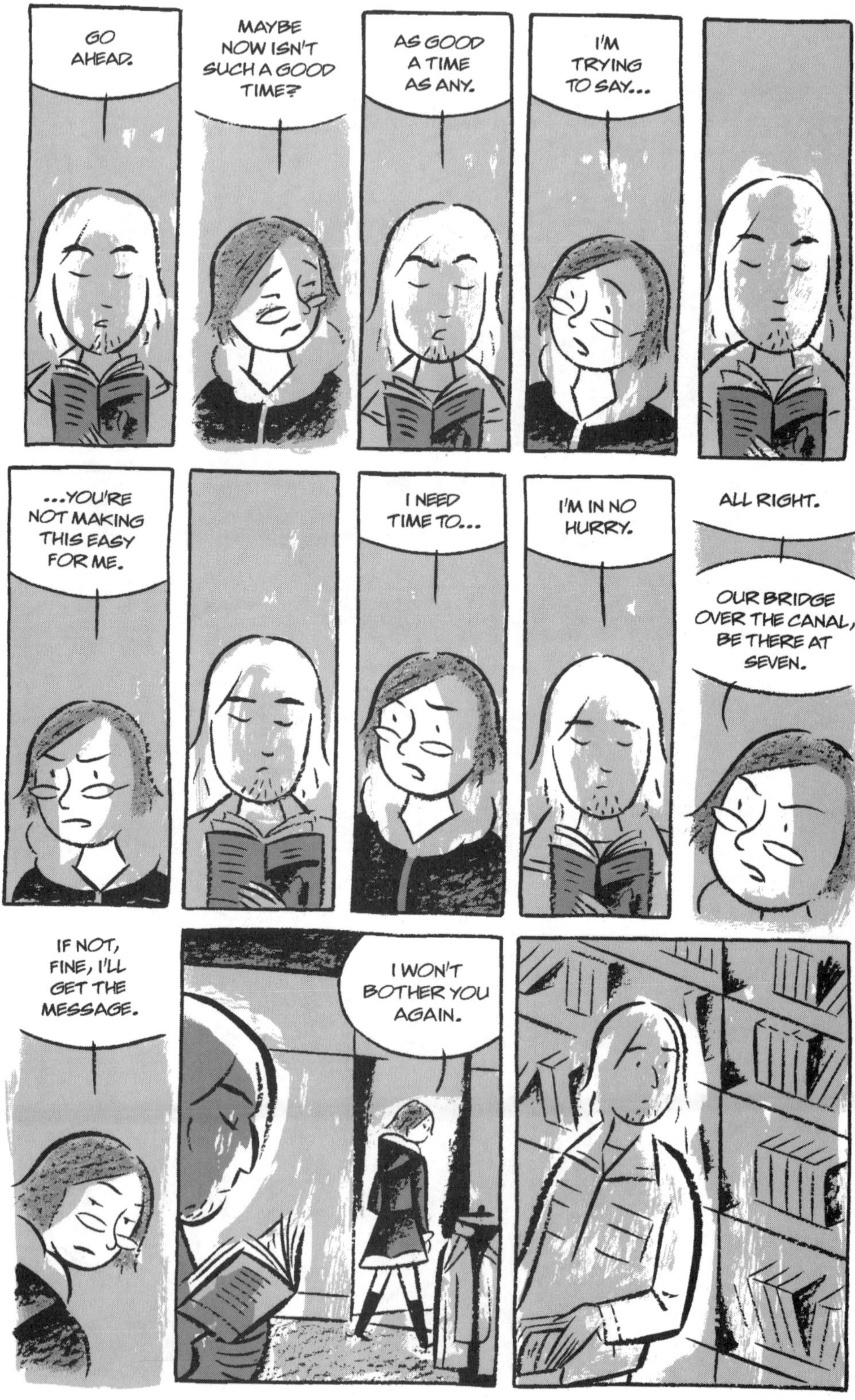
GO AHEAD.
MAYBE NOW ISN'T SUCH A GOOD TIME?
AS GOOD A TIME AS ANY.
I'M TRYING TO SAY...
...YOU'RE NOT MAKING THIS EASY FOR ME.
I NEED TIME TO...
I'M IN NO HURRY.
ALL RIGHT.
OUR BRIDGE OVER THE CANAL, BE THERE AT SEVEN.
IF NOT, FINE, I'LL GET THE MESSAGE.
I WON'T BOTHER YOU AGAIN.

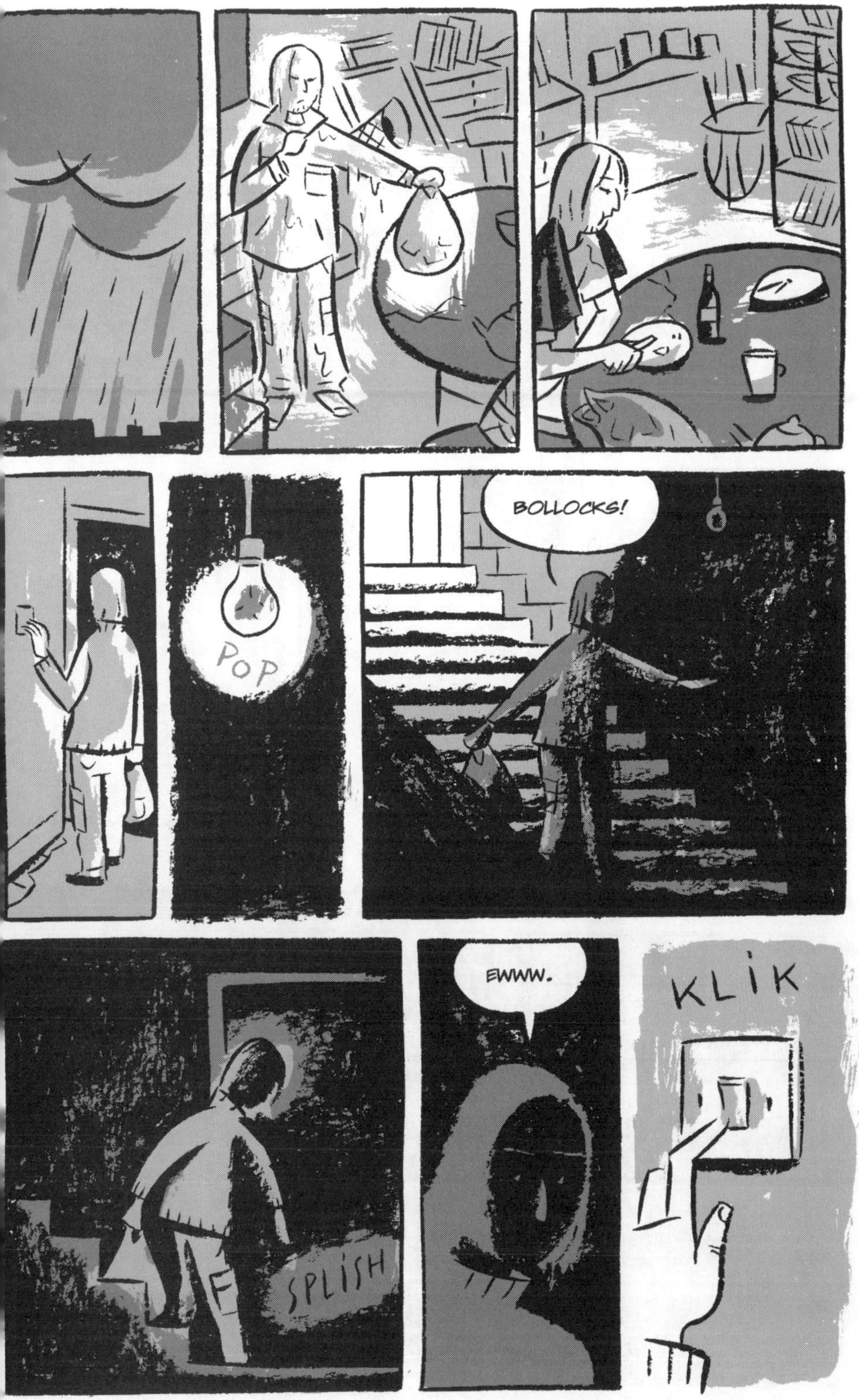
POP
BOLLOCKS!
SPLISH
EWWW.
KLIK

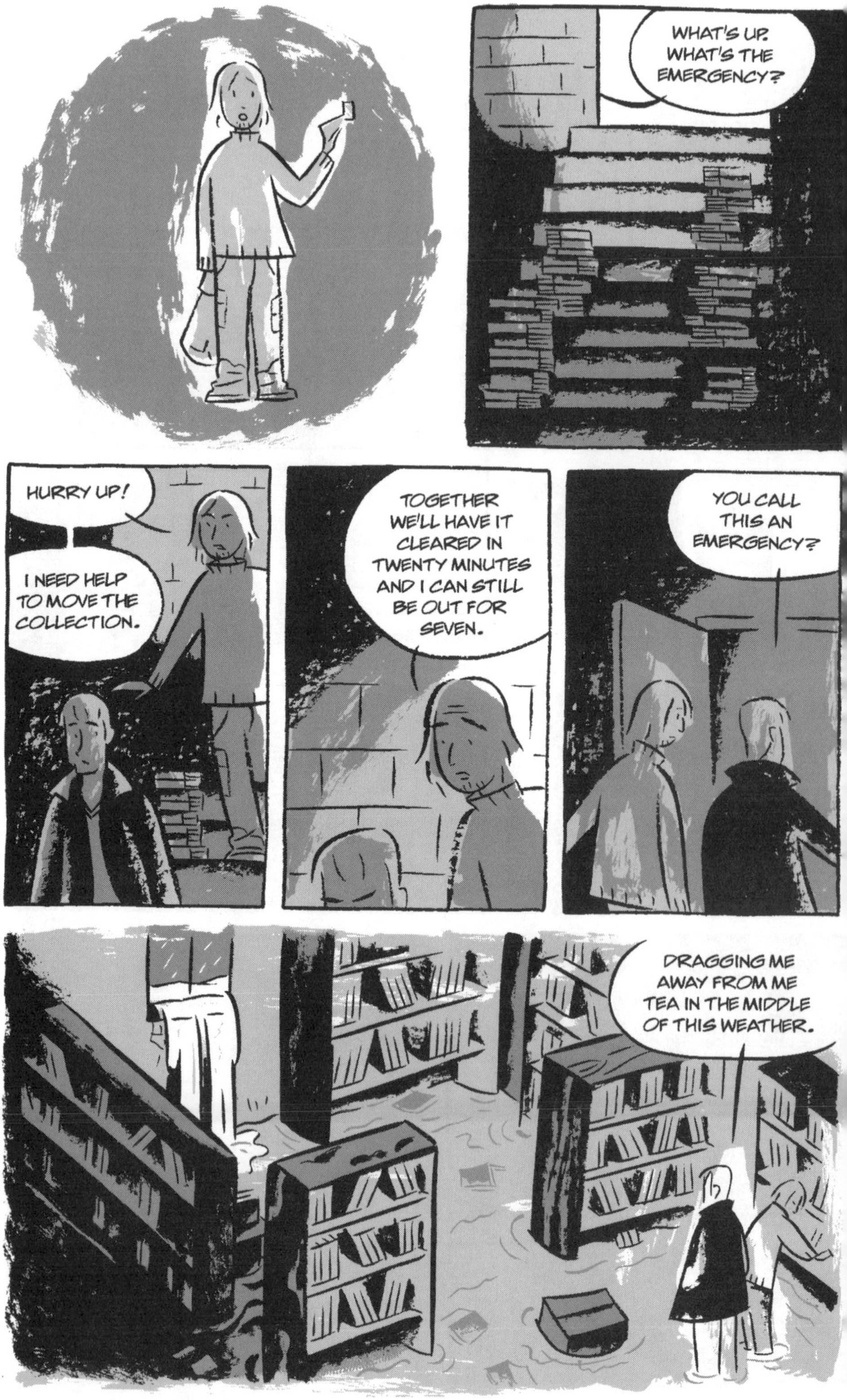
WHAT'S UP. WHAT'S THE EMERGENCY?
HURRY UP!
I NEED HELP TO MOVE THE COLLECTION.
TOGETHER WE'LL HAVE IT CLEARED IN TWENTY MINUTES AND I CAN STILL BE OUT FOR SEVEN.
YOU CALL THIS AN EMERGENCY?
DRAGGING ME AWAY FROM ME TEA IN THE MIDDLE OF THIS WEATHER.

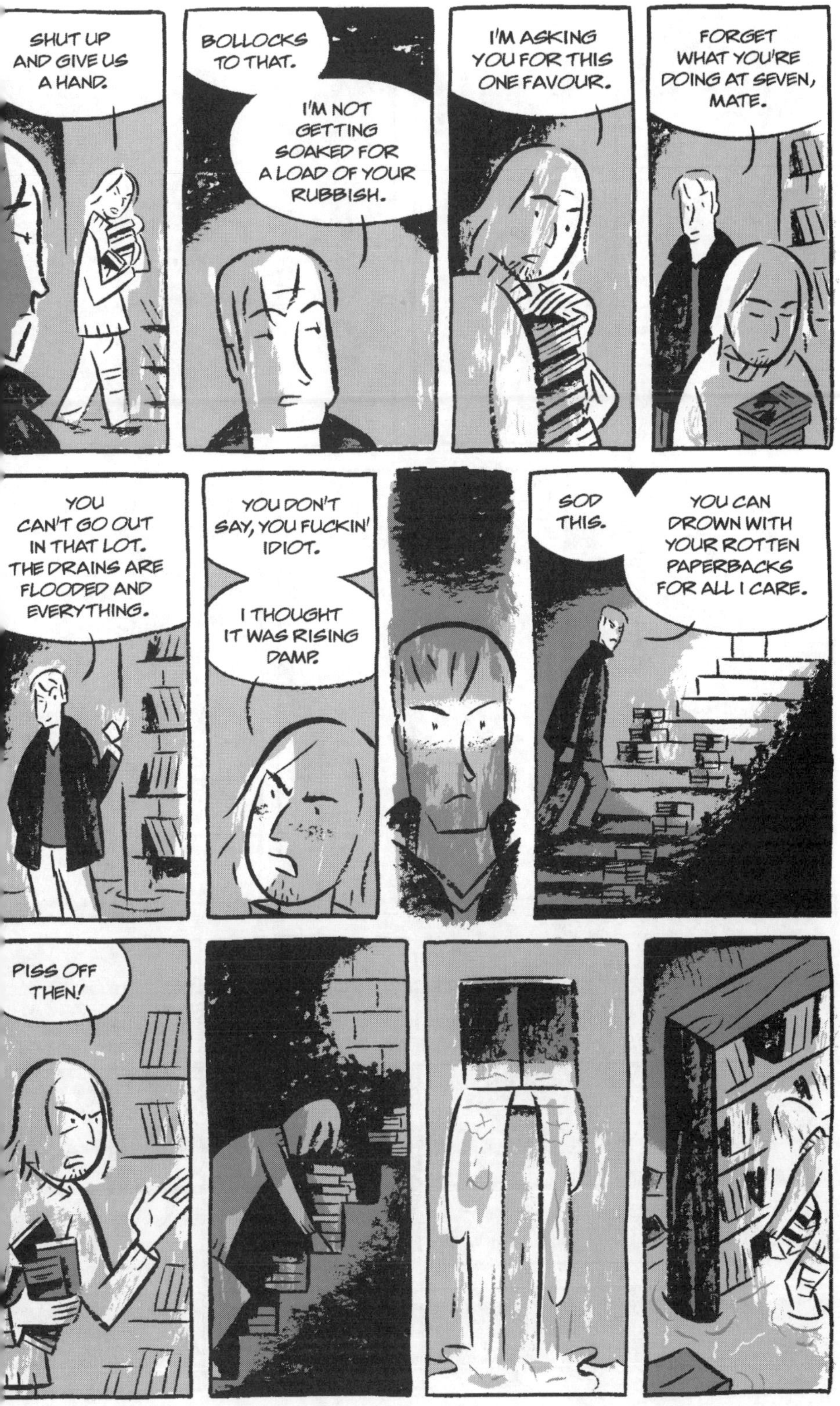
SHUT UP AND GIVE US A HAND.
BOLLOCKS TO THAT.
I'M NOT GETTING SOAKED FOR A LOAD OF YOUR RUBBISH.
I'M ASKING YOU FOR THIS ONE FAVOUR.
FORGET WHAT YOU'RE DOING AT SEVEN, MATE.
YOU CAN'T GO OUT IN THAT LOT. THE DRAINS ARE FLOODED AND EVERYTHING.
YOU DON'T SAY, YOU FUCKIN' IDIOT.
I THOUGHT IT WAS RISING DAMP.
SOD THIS.
YOU CAN DROWN WITH YOUR ROTTEN PAPERBACKS FOR ALL I CARE.
PISS OFF THEN!

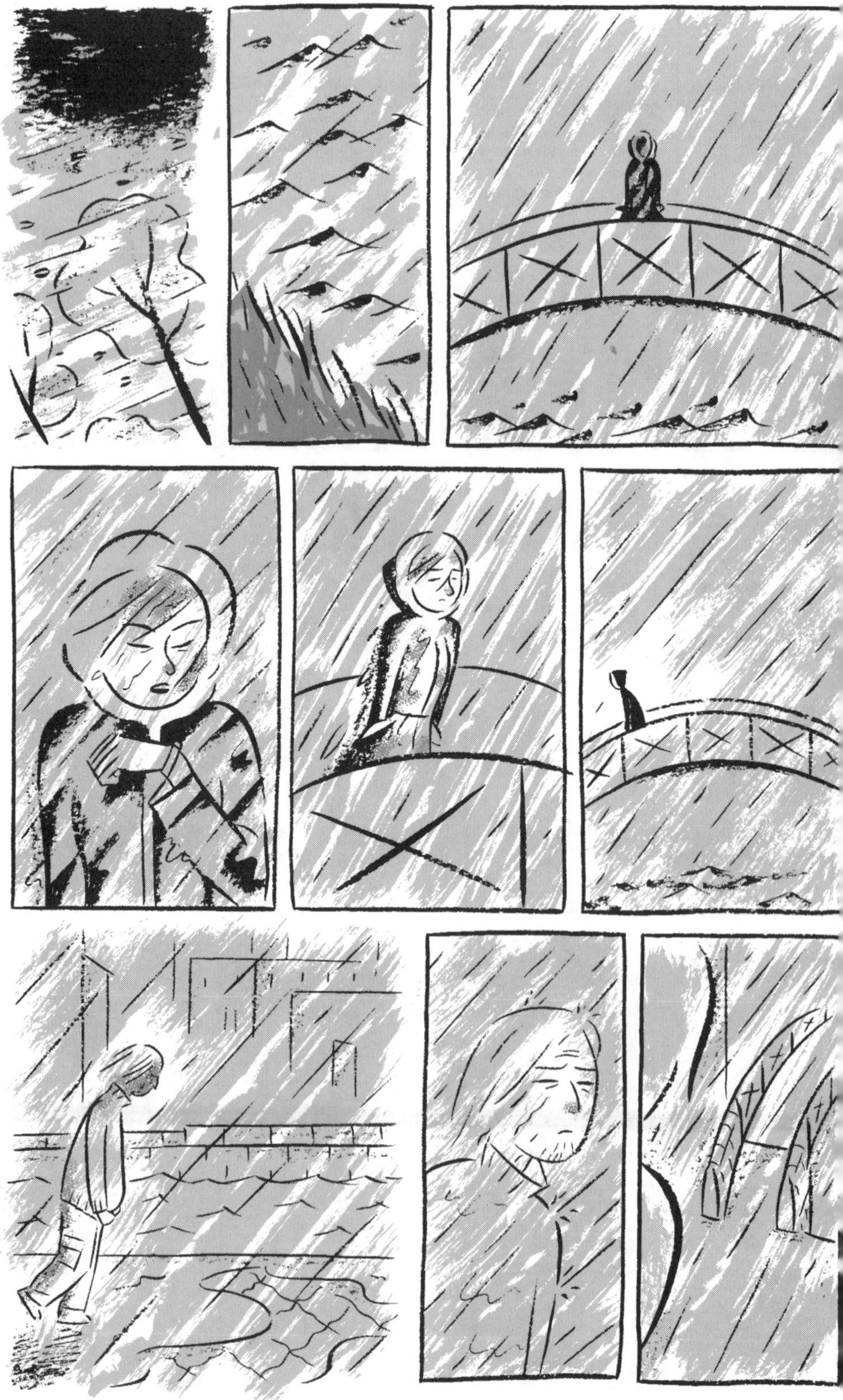

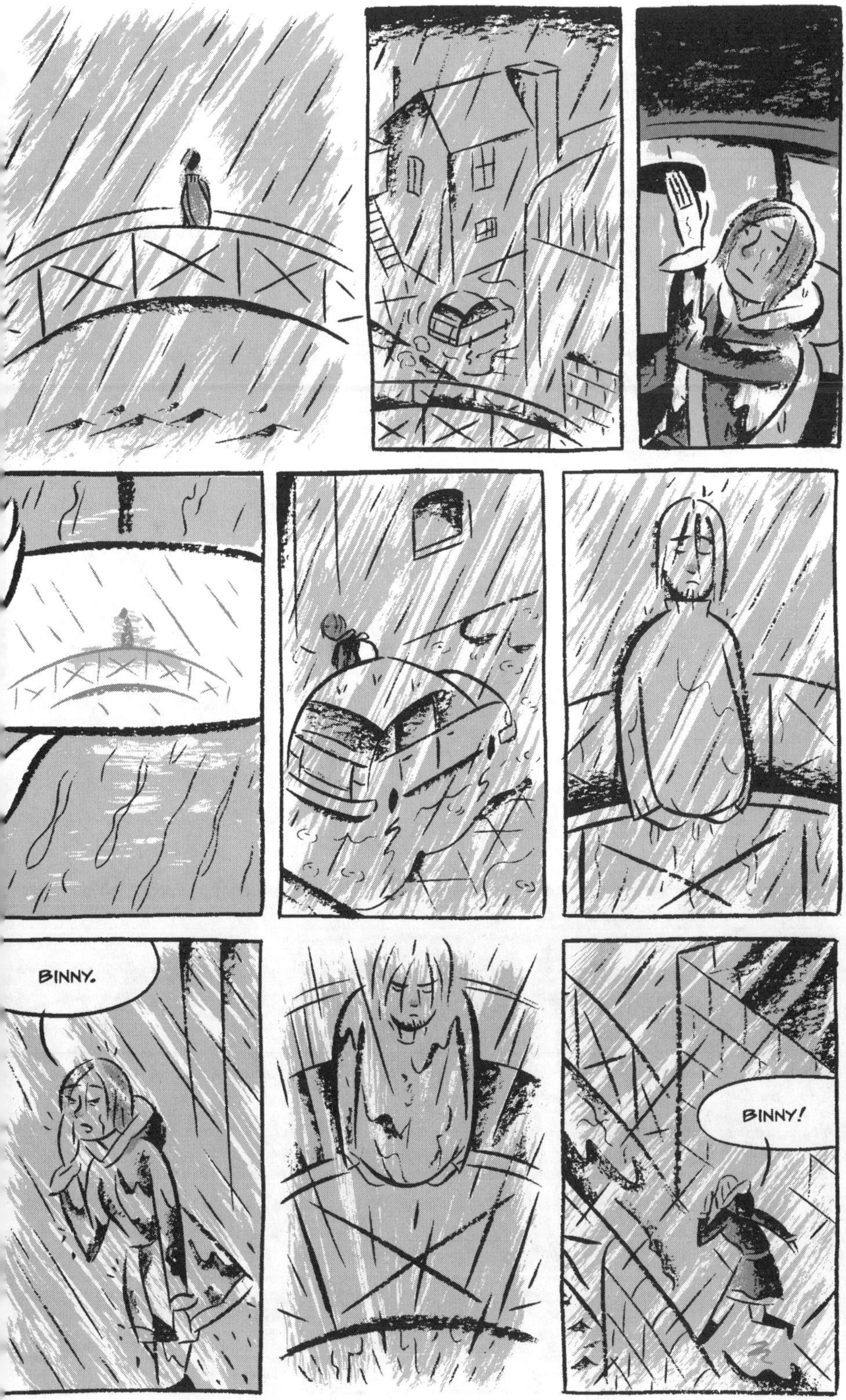
BINNY.
BINNY!

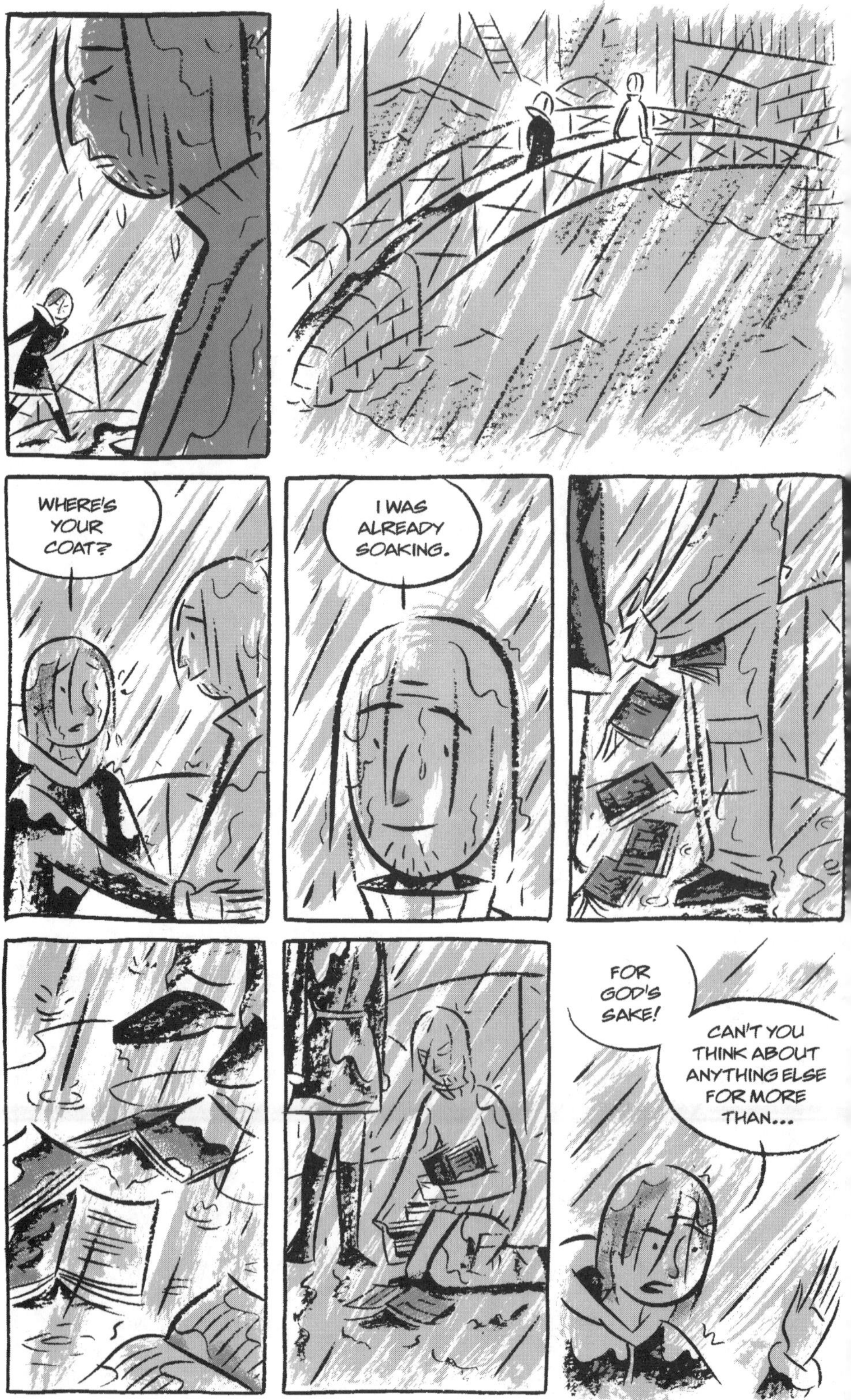
WHERE'S YOUR COAT?
I WAS ALREADY SOAKING.
FOR GOD'S SAKE!
CAN'T YOU THINK ABOUT ANYTHING ELSE FOR MORE THAN...

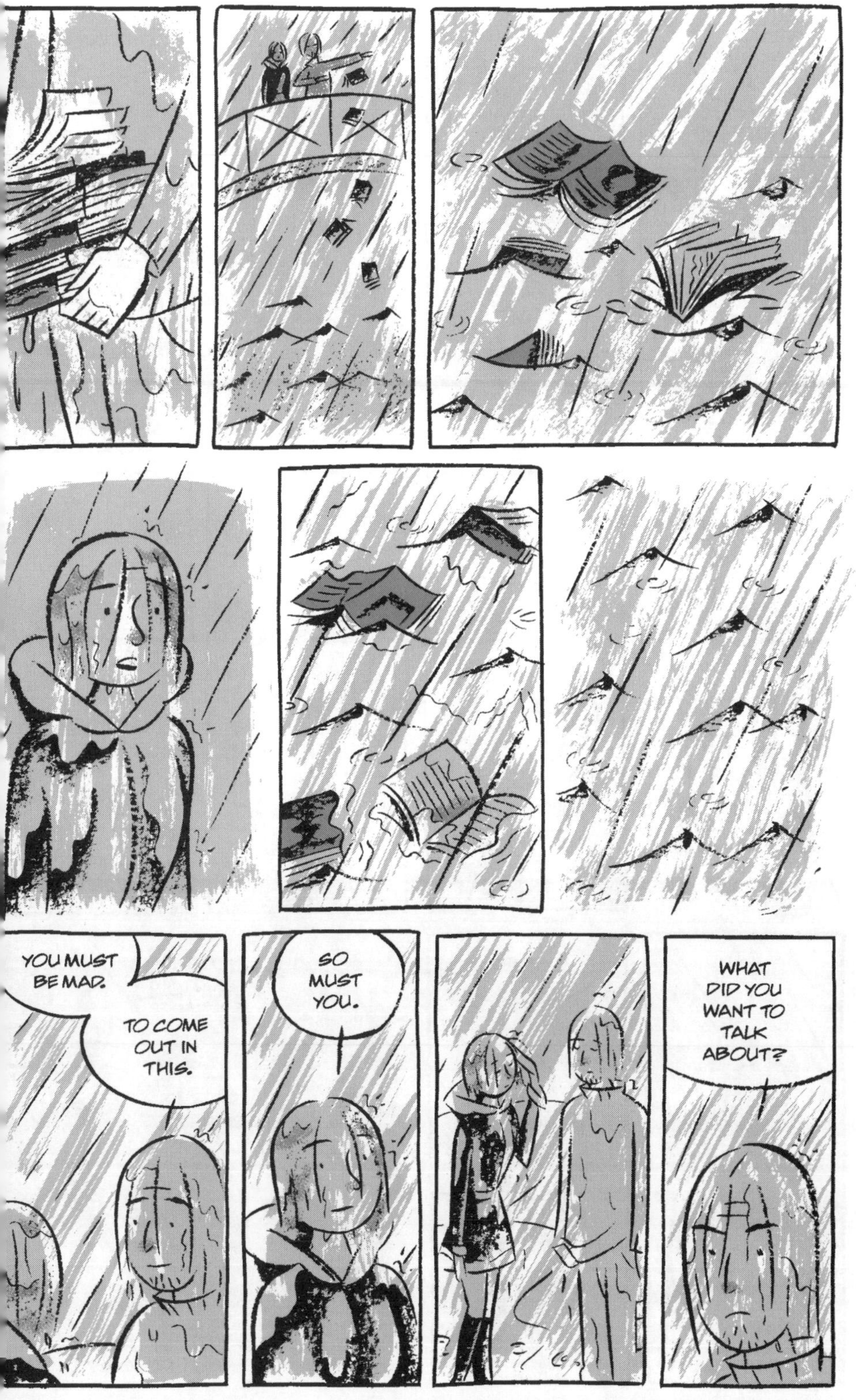
YOU MUST BE MAD.
TO COME OUT IN THIS.
SO MUST YOU.
WHAT DID YOU WANT TO TALK ABOUT?

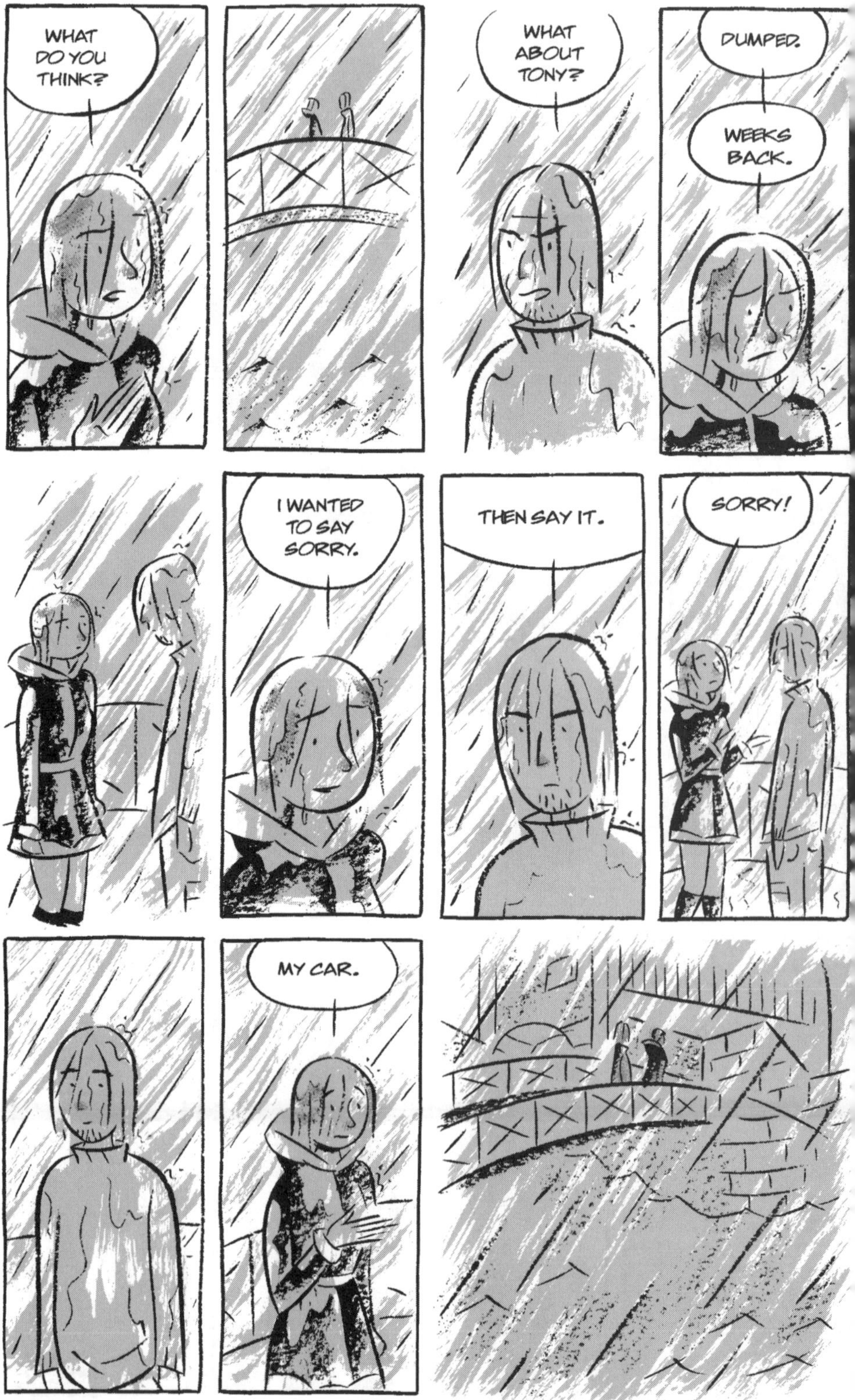
WHAT DO YOU THINK?
WHAT ABOUT TONY?
DUMPED.
WEEKS BACK.
I WANTED TO SAY SORRY.
THEN SAY IT.
SORRY!
MY CAR.

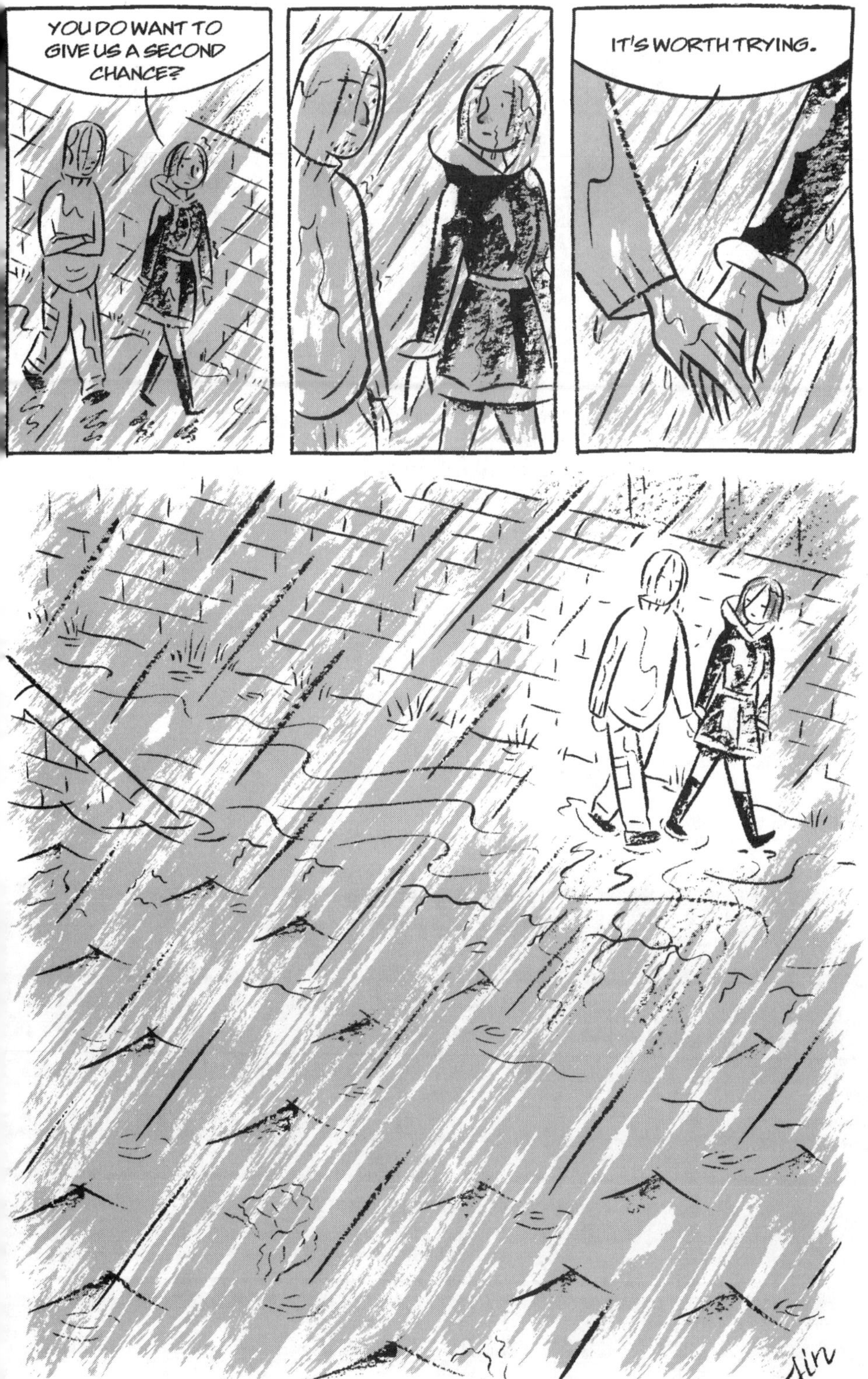
YOU DO WANT TO GIVE US A SECOND CHANCE?
IT'S WORTH TRYING.
Jin

città di Torino   Provincia Di Torino   Regione Piemonte

This book was created to coincide with the Big Torino 2002—the International Biennial of Young Arts held in Turin, Italy. The festival was established to celebrate artists under the age of thirty-five. Visit the festival online at www.bigtorino.net.

Published by Oni Press, Inc.
joe nozemack, publisher
jamie s. rich, editor in chief
james lucas jones, associate editor

ONI PRESS, INC.
6336 SE Milwaukie Avenue, PMB30
Portland, OR 97202
USA

www.onipress.com
www.andiwatson.com

First edition: April 2002
ISBN 1-929998-41-4

1 3 5 7 9 10 8 6 4 2
PRINTED IN CANADA